THE STORY OF

SCOTCH WHISKY

"To Elsa, Flora, Chloe, Molly and especially Kitty"

AUTHOR'S ACKNOWLEDGMENTS

I woud like to thank the following people: Geraldine Coates, Charlie Maclean, Dave Broom, Gavin Smith, Rosemary Gallacher, Christine McCafferty and the late Michael Jackson. I would also like to thank the long-suffering staff at Carlton Books, not least my editor: Martin Corteel.

First published in 2015 as *The Treasures of Scotch Whisky*

This edition published in 2017 by Carlton Books Limited
A division of the Carlton Publishing Group
20 Mortimer Street, London W1T 3JW

A CIP catalogue for this book is available from the British Library

Editorial Manager: Martin Corteel
Design Manager: Luke Griffin
Design: Namkwan Cho, www.gradedesign.com
Picture Research: Paul Langan
Production: Lisa Cook

ISBN: 978 1 78739 020 1

Printed and bound in China

THE STORY OF

SCOTCH WHISKY

**A JOURNEY OF DISCOVERY INTO THE
WORLD'S NOBLEST SPIRIT**

TOM BRUCE-GARDYNE

CARLTON
BOOKS

CONTENTS

INTRODUCTION

UNLIKE MANY DRINKS, THERE IS NO INSTANT GRATIFICATION WITH SCOTCH WHISKY. FEW IF ANY OF US WERE SMITTEN BY OUR FIRST SIP, AND THE SWEETNESS OFTEN THERE ON THE NOSE CAN BE HARD TO FIND ON THE TONGUE. TO THE UNINITIATED, THERE IS SOMETHING ALMOST PRIMAL ABOUT SINGLE MALTS WITH THEIR RAW, PUNGENT, BITTERSWEET CHARACTER AND THAT'S TRUE OF MANY BLENDS, TOO. BUT AS WHISKY LOVERS KNOW, IT IS WORTH PERSEVERING UNTIL YOU ARE WELL AND TRULY SEDUCED BY THIS STRANGE BREW.

The story of Scotland's national drink is equally compelling, and goes back hundreds of years. While the first recorded mention is from the late fifteenth century, the origins of whisky are surely older still, and it is tempting to believe it was at least partly born of necessity. As well as being a drink to share, whisky was something to rub on aching joints, cleanse wounds, act as an antibiotic and numb the pain of a long, Scottish winter. Was the water of life discovered by accident by the Scots, or did those Irish monks bring more than Christianity with them in their coracles ... who knows?

This book will lead you on a journey through the drink's evolution from a wild, hairy-arsed spirit hot from the still to modern-day whisky mellowed in wood. We will pause to consider the production process and ponder how a few humble ingredients – just water, malted barley and a sprinkling of yeast, in the case of malts, can produce something so infinitely diverse and complex. Then it is out to the whisky regions to see how each developed its own identity, before delving into the key malt distilleries themselves.

The third part of the book explores how whisky has soaked its way into popular culture through books, films and music hall. Scotch added true grit to countless pulp fiction heroes and an air of sophistication to Hollywood stars who in turn helped promote it to a wider audience. It also seeped into the poetry of Robert Burns, who happily confessed it to be his muse and appreciated its earthy charms, perhaps better than anyone, so it is only fitting that Burns Night should be a raucous, whisky-fuelled celebration of his life.

The Scotch Whisky Story also aims to celebrate this most beguiling spirit in images as much as words by including a wealth of illustrations and some fascinating documents that you can take out and peruse. With a colourful past stretching back over five centuries, there is a rich archive to plunder and reproduce to help bring the story alive. All that is missing is the most vital ingredient of all, but you can rectify that yourself. With a freshly poured dram in one hand and the book in the other, hopefully you will be in for a treat.

Tom Bruce-Gardyne,
Edinburgh, May 2017

HOW WHISKY IS MADE

TO MAKE WHISKY YOU FIRST HAVE TO MAKE BEER, AND ANY DISTILLERY VISIT WILL LEAD YOU BY THE NOSE FROM THE BEERY AROMAS OF A BREWERY TO THE SWEET SCENT OF DISTILLATION. BUT BEFORE THAT YOU WILL LEARN ABOUT THE INGREDIENTS, STARTING WITH WATER, WHICH IS USED TO STEEP THE BARLEY, MAKE THE MASH, CONDENSE THE SPIRIT AND REDUCE ITS STRENGTH FOR MATURATION AND AGAIN AT THE TIME OF BOTTLING UNLESS IT IS A CASK-STRENGTH WHISKY. WITHOUT WATER THERE WOULD BE NO WATER OF LIFE, YET WHETHER IT IS HARD OR SOFT, TINGED WITH PEAT OR CRYSTAL CLEAR, ITS IMPACT ON FLAVOUR IS MARGINAL.

For malt whisky the grain is always barley, much of it from Scotland's East Coast barley belt that runs from the Black Isle to the Borders. The whisky industry uses various strains of barley, but the choice is more about maximizing alcoholic yield than influencing taste. First the grain is plunged into a cold bath where it doubles in size, and traditionally it was then spread out on a stone malting floor for a week as it began to sprout little rootlets and begin germinating. The grain had to be turned twice a day by men with wooden shovels to prevent it matting together. Today, apart from a few distilleries like Bowmore and Highland Park, the process is done entirely by industrial maltings. What remains critical, however, is whether the kilns to dry the grain use peat or not. Peat is partially decomposed vegetable matter – grass, heather, gorse and the like, that has been slowly compacted into a hard black layer over thousands of years. Only when lit does it release its pungent, bittersweet aroma that seeps into the malted barley as its blue smoke wafts up from the kiln. By mixing the ratio of peated to unpeated malt, the distiller can determine the peatiness, or phenolic content, of the finished whisky.

The malt is ground to a coarse grist and mixed with hot water in a large, circular mash-tun with rotating rakes to prevent it clogging. The aim is to extract all the soluble sugars, and three separate mashes are needed, each one progressively hotter. What is left is compressed into cattle cake, while the liquid is drained off into large wooden vessels called washbacks, having been injected with yeast. Here it ferments to a cloudy brew of around 8 per cent alcohol that some of the more hardened distillery workers used to drink by the pint. The wash, as it is now called, is filled into a wash still – basically a towering copper kettle – and heated for a first distillation. The component parts of the wash are teased apart thanks to their different boiling points. The wash still takes the alcoholic strength to around 21 per cent, which is then trebled in a second distillation

in the spirit still. If you are Irish, or that way inclined, you would distil it a third time to produce a slightly lighter spirit, though twice is enough for most Scots. Stills have always been made of copper, which reacts with the boiling liquid and helps strip out some of the impurities. The more copper contact as the vapours rise up the still and then condense back down, the cleaner the spirit will be. This explains why the shape of the still and rate of distillation help to make every single malt unique.

The vapours that make it over the top of the still then travel down the copper pipe known as the lyne arm to be condensed, either in a modern condenser or an old-fashioned worm tub. The liquid then flows through the spirit safe, a glass-fronted box of polished brass. The stillman rejects the volatile alcohols, or foreshots, until the spirit is deemed worth collecting. Half an hour later, as the strength slowly falls, the feints appear and these too are rejected. The middle part, or cut, is the new-make spirit and represents a balance of clean alcohols and impurities. Though toxic in a higher dose these impurities, or congeners, give a whisky its distillery character and add an extra kick to any resulting hangover.

Most distillery tours end with a dram and a visit to the distillery shop, with perhaps a cursory glimpse at a warehouse. Slumbering in the dark, row upon row of casks seem to be doing not very much at all, yet it is here where the real magic occurs. A clear, raw spirit is transformed over the years into a mellow golden whisky, picking up colour as well as certain flavours from the oak. Breathing in air and exhaling alcohol through the pores in the wood, the whisky loses its rough edges and gains complexity in a way that's still not fully understood. Maturation may be the most mystical and uncontrollable part of the process, but it determines perhaps two-thirds of a whisky's character.

BELOW Crystal clear newmake spirit flows through the spirits safe at Laphroaig on Islay.

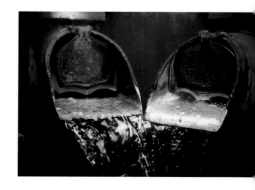

The rules on maturation – at least three years in an oak cask – only came in a century ago, and prior to that most whisky would have been a rough, immature spirit. There was little incentive for prolonged ageing with whisky losing up to two per cent a year in evaporation – the so-called "angels' share". The industry relied on second-hand European oak wine barrels, particularly sherry casks which were plentiful given the drink's popularity and the fact it was nearly all shipped in bulk. Gradually sherry casks have been replaced by American oak ex-bourbon barrels that now account for 90 per cent of the industry's needs. A first-fill sherry butt (500 litres) will give the whisky a spicy, resinous fruitcake character, compared to the sweeter coconut and vanilla notes of its bourbon equivalent at half the size. As of 2015 the former cost from €750 (£550), compared to US$130 (£85) for the latter. The type of oak, whether American or European, the previous contents, the length of maturation and whether the cask is a "first-fill" (i.e. never previously used for Scotch) all play a part. A first-fill cask will imbue more colour and flavour in five years than a third-fill in twenty or thirty.

BELOW Pot stills come in almost as many shapes as there are distilleries. This determines the amount of copper contact during distillation which in turn will influence the purity and flavour of the spirit.

NEXT PAGES Without barley scotch whisky would not be the same.

PART ONE

THE HISTORY OF SCOTCH WHISKY

MONKS AND FRIARS

WHEN, SOME TWENTY YEARS AGO, THE SCOTCH WHISKY INDUSTRY CELEBRATED ITS FIVE HUNDREDTH ANNIVERSARY, IT TRACED ITS BIRTH TO A TERSE NOTE IN THE EXCHEQUER ROLLS OF 1494: "TO FRIAR JOHN COR, BY ORDER OF THE KING, TO MAKE ACQUA VITAE VIII BOLLS OF MALT." THE FRIAR FROM LINDORES ABBEY IN FIFE WAS CLEARLY DISTILLING ON SOME SCALE. EIGHT BOLLS OF MALT WOULD MAKE YOU MORE THAN A FEW HUNDRED BOTTLES OF SCOTCH WHISKY TODAY.

This may be the first recorded mention of *aqua vitae*, the water of life, but as the whisky writer Charles Maclean says, "it raises as many questions as it answers". It tells us that by the end of the fifteenth century distillation had reached Scotland, but not when it began, nor whether it was being drunk, used in medicine or perfume, or even gunpowder. The history of whisky as we know it might be younger than we thought; or, more likely, considerably older.

The secret of distillation spread from Ancient China via India and the Middle East. By the fourth century BC, Aristotle was distilling water by boiling sea water and collecting the steam in balls of wool suspended above it. It was hardly alcohol, but it shared the same principle of applying heat to a body or mass in order to release its essence or "spirit", which would then condense back into a purified form. The discovery of distillation also mirrored the alchemists' quest for the mythical quintessence that could transform base metal into gold – an obvious fascination for a man like King James IV, who was deeply into science and often deeply in debt.

While the light of knowledge from Arab and Greek scholars was mostly snuffed out during the Dark Ages, it flickered on in Irish monasteries. It is therefore tempting to believe that Irish monks brought more than Christianity with them when they sailed across to Scotland in their coracles. The

LEFT The ruins of Lindores Abbey in Fife and spiritual home of Scotch whisky where Friar John Cor was granted the right to make *aqua vitae* in 1494. The abbey was sacked in 1559 at the behest of John Knox.

ABOVE The famous Exchequer Roll of 1494 with the first ever written reference to distillation in Scotland. Presumably the "acqua vitae" was for drinking rather than medicine or for making gunpowder, but we can never be completely sure.

McBeatha family from Ireland may well have known the secret when they became the hereditary physicians to the Lord of the Isles in around 1300.

Then again, perhaps whisky was simply discovered by accident by the Scots themselves. Beer had been brewed in Scotland since neolithic times, and whisky is nothing if not distilled beer. Perhaps, in an effort to rescue some heather ale that had turned sour, someone decided to boil it up. Maybe a few droplets of vapour condensed to give a glimpse of what became the national spirit?

MAKING MEN MERRY

Whenever it happened, the secret of this magic brew soon spread. It was certainly a wonder drug in the view of Peter Morwyng, who wrote one of the first books on distilling in 1559. Besides being a cure for tired eyes, palsy, poor memory, ringworm and spots, he decreed: "It is mervelous profitable for frantic man and such as be melancholy ... It taketh away sadness, pensiveness; it maketh men merri, witti and encreaseth audacitie."

By 1579 distilling had become sufficiently mainstream to provoke fears of a grain shortage. That year an Act of the Scottish Parliament restricted the practice to "Earls, Lords, Barons and Gentlemen for their own use". In 1609 James VI of Scotland (James I

of England) attempted to impose order on the Western Isles through the Statutes of Iona, which shows how whisky was becoming a commercial trade. It blamed "the great poverty of the isles" on people's "inordinate love of strong wines and acquavite, which they purchased partly from dealers among

TOP King James I of England (and James VI of Scotland) battled to impose his will on the wild and intemperate Western Isles through the Statutes of Iona in 1609.

LEFT Samuel Johnson and his friend and biographer, James Boswell, in Edinburgh before setting out on their epic Highland tour in 1773 that was published two years later as a "Journey to the Western Islands of Scotland".

themselves, [and] partly from merchants belonging to the mainland". Unless they happened to be "barons or wealthy gentlemen", they were ordered to rely on their own stills and not buy from the mainland.

The fear of the chaos unleashed by "strong wines and acquavite", and the desire to control and tax them, became a common refrain of government. In 1644 the first excise duty was imposed, and though a temporary tax it was not long before the State became used to this sweet source of revenue. Within 20 years, the first "gaugers" (excisemen) had appeared on the scene, with the power to enter any "distilling house" and collect duty. Meanwhile explorers to the far-flung reaches of the Highlands and Islands reported back with awe at the strength and quantity of spirits consumed. Visiting Mull, Martin Martin wrote that "the natives are accustomed to take a large dose of acquavite as a corrective against the climate" – a tradition that doubtless continues.

On the Black Isle at Ferintosh, near Dingwall, Duncan Forbes III was Scotland's first known commercial distiller. The scale of production can be gauged from his massive £54,000 bid for compensation when the Jacobites burned down "his brewery of acqua vitae" in 1689. Instead of paying, the Scottish Parliament offered him virtually tax-free distilling so long as he used grain from his own land.

WHAT IS THIS … WHISKY?

It was not until the 1730s that we find mention of "whiskie". One of the earliest references was a letter from Bailie John Steuart of Inverness to his brother-in-law urging him to "keep a sober regular dyet" and "forbear drinking that poisonous drink, I mean drams of brandie and whiskie". The word was a corruption of *uiskie* or *uisge beatha* – the Scots Gaelic translation of *aqua vitae*, the water of life.

The word "Usquebaugh" appears in Dr Johnson's famous dictionary of 1755 with the following definition: "It is a compounded distilled spirit, being drawn on aromaticks; and the Irish sort is particularly distinguished for its pleasant and mild flavour. The Highland sort is somewhat hotter; and, by corruption, in Scottish they call it whisky."

The Forbes family extended their estate, built three distilleries and were making profits of over £2 million by 1784 when the State finally ended the concession. By then, it is said, Ferintosh accounted for almost two-thirds of all the legal whisky in Scotland, and it was clearly a serious brand, for its passing was mourned by Robert Burns, who penned the lines: "Thee Ferintosh! O sadly lost! Scotland lament frae coast to coast!"

BELOW This extract from "Canedolia" by the late poet, Edwin Morgan, is carved into the wall of the Scottish Parliament in Edinburgh. "A wee ferintosh" refers to what was Scotland's oldest commercial distillery on the Black Isle.

BELOW LEFT The secret of distillation spread from Ancient China via India and the Middle East. By the fourth century BC, it had reached Ancient Greece.

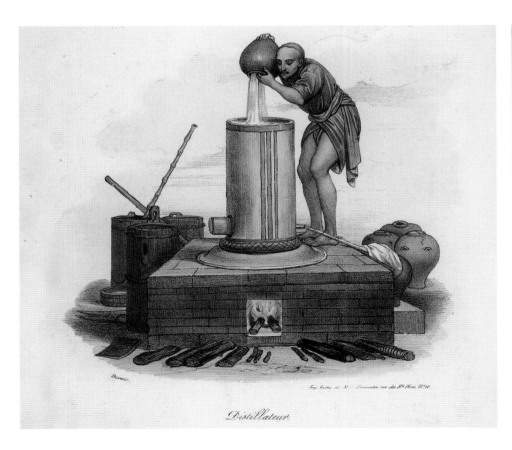

Distillateur

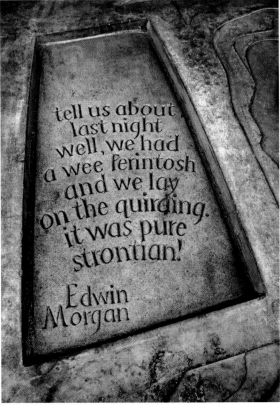

tell us about last night well, we had a wee ferintosh and we lay on the quirang. it was pure strontian!

Edwin Morgan

UNION, REVOLT ... AND EXCISE

WHEN THE UNION BETWEEN ENGLAND AND SCOTLAND WAS FORMED IN 1707, FUNDS WERE NEEDED URGENTLY TO PAY FOR IT, AND A KEY SOURCE OF REVENUE WAS TO BE THE TAXATION OF DRINK.

At first the Hanoverian regime trod extremely carefully, as though sensing trouble. A Board of Excise was set up in Edinburgh, but it was not until 10 years after successfully crushing the first Jacobite revolt in 1715 that the authorities dared to double the tax on malt. Although it was still only half that of England, it provoked a brewery strike in Edinburgh and a full-scale riot in Glasgow that left 11 dead and the house of Daniel Campbell, the city's MP, burned to the ground. With the £6,000 he was paid in compensation, Campbell bought Islay and played a key role in developing distilling on the island.

The Malt Tax of 1725 hit beer harder than whisky, which in those days would have been a very inconsistent spirit to say the least. It was seldom, if ever, allowed to mellow in wood, and would have been drunk raw and almost hot from the still. No wonder it was often compounded with heather, herbs, wild berries and honey to help it slip down. It was around this time that the first licensed distillers began to

BELOW The Battle of Culloden of 1746 crushed the second Jacobite uprising under Charles Edward Stuart, "Bonnie Prince Charlie". The brutal repression of Highland culture that followed, including the banning of kilts and bagpipes, helped turn whisky into the spirit of defiance.

crop up in the Lowlands, among them John Stein at Kennetpans in Clackmannanshire.

Stein had four sons who all became distillers and a daughter who married John Haig – another whisky dynasty. Together with a third distilling family, the Phelpses, they came to represent whisky's industrial revolution and were to some extent a Lowland mafia compared to their rustic Highland cousins. The Steins' Kilbagie distillery was the biggest in Scotland when it was built in the 1770s and had a workforce of over 300. It produced so much draff from the distilling process that it was said to feed 7,000 black cattle and 2,000 sheep.

CROSSING THE LINE

After the Battle of Culloden in 1746, when the second Jacobite rebellion was crushed, the government banned bagpipes and the wearing of tartan.

This deliberate attack on Highland culture only added to the allure of whisky, whose production grew with each attempt to tax and control it. As the Irish said of poteen, illicit Scotch was: "superior in sweetness, salubriety and gusto to all that machinery, science and capital can produce in the legalized way".

By 1760 it was claimed that licensed distilleries accounted for only a tenth of all the whisky drunk in Scotland. The rest came from private stills which gurgled away in every corner of the country from the furthest-flung farmstead to the city centre. In Edinburgh it was said there were 400 stills of which only eight were licensed. There had always been smuggling, but it began to surge after a series of disastrous harvests prompted a ban on distilling in 1756.

A further run of poor harvests in the 1780s highlighted the tension between feeding the masses

BELOW "The Illicit Highland Whisky Still" by Edwin Landseer (c.1829) is a classic, romanticized depiction of whisky. The Highlander in his bothey astride a dead stag with his bare-footed bairns, and a small, copper still bubbling away in the background.

and supplying an increasingly voracious whisky industry. When the mob turned up at James Haig's Edinburgh distillery of Canonmills, he had to assure them he was not storing any carrots, turnips or peas to make his whisky. Meanwhile the government finally banned private stills, though probably to little effect, and brought in new laws that split the country in two when it came to whisky.

The Wash Act of 1784 allowed distillers north of a line from the Firth of Clyde to the Firth of Tay to use much smaller stills and pay less tax than Lowland distillers, who were naturally upset. The fact that Highland whisky was theoretically banned south of the line was little consolation given the scale of smuggling that was going on. Indeed, because the new tax regime encouraged those in the Lowlands to run their large, flat-bottomed stills ever faster, demand for the somewhat gentler Highland whisky only increased.

Lowland stills were being worked at ferocious speed, with all manner of ugly flavours and impurities finding their way into the finished drink. By the late 1770s, the Steins had discovered a whole new market in England – not for whisky, but for raw spirit that was rectified into gin. In just five years this trade jumped from 2,000 to 184,000 gallons, prompting a vicious price war with the London distillers who successfully lobbied Westminster to ramp up the duty on Scottish spirit. When the Lowland distillers were then told to give 12 months' notice of intent to export, the Haig–Stein empire collapsed with massive debts. In time the two families recovered and rose again with the advent of continuous distillation in the 1820s.

By 1800 four-fifths of legal Scotch whisky came from the Lowlands, from 31 licensed distilleries, almost half the number in the Highlands which tended to be much smaller. Below the surface the trade in illicit whisky began to surge, encouraged by periodic bans on distilling and by every tax increase. It was smuggled southwards along the old drove roads used for taking cattle from upland pastures to be sold in the big markets like Falkirk. Facing the smugglers was a thinly stretched, hopelessly outnumbered body of excisemen, or gaugers. It was an unequal battle, as Thomas Guthrie, minister of Brechin in Angus, makes clear in his account (above) of smugglers coming to town.

The DEADLY GROANS of the *WHISKY STILLS*. who were condemned to suffer Martyrdom on the 17th of this present month of July 1795, for the horrid and bloody murder of starving above 200,000 professed Christians in this island.

With the sorrowful Lamentation of all the Dram-Drinkers.

COME all ye that are fond of me, it is to you that I now for this time address myself, Oh my dear friends, you have no doubt, heard of the fatal stroke that I am about to receive on the 17th of this present month, and in order that you may pity me now under the sentence of almost total annihilation from society, especially those of my greatest admirers; Oh, my dear friends, what will now become of you, who clasped me into your very bosom every morning! you will no more court me upon so easy terms as you have hitherto done.

It will be necessary, in order that you may condole with me, that you know my name and designation; it is true I have got a great many names, or as I should rather call them nick-names, which differ very materially from that which I first had, which was Aquavitae, or more properly speaking the water of life; the name I generally go by at this day is WHISKY, a name which differs very much from the original of my origin; but those who were my real friends, always gave me a new name, which I the more readily put up with, as I knew them to be my real admirers, and it now gives me the greatest affliction, that I must be forever banished from the society of all those, who took so much delight in my company, and was always happy, when they had me standing on the table before them. My friend would say to his neighbour, will you take a dram, or will you take a caulker, or will you taste the blue this morning, you will be much the better of it; and if my friend and lover got his neighbour to partake of me it was rarely that he lost any thing by introducing me to his acquaintance, for I very often was returned with new strength, and I was swallowed up with the greatest delight in mouthfuls; and such as were dumb, I made them speak with the greatest ease by the time I had touched their tongue with half a dozen of fills of my little christal jacket, my dear could talk of politicks, and the weighty affairs of state, with the greatest volatility, and ease. I then could beat the French with big words & strange grimaces.

Our wise legislators, who are no doubt, possessed with a great deal of wisdom have sat upon me, tried and condemned me to six months annihilation, not for any crime that they found in me, but that I was destructive to that poor diminitive grain called Barley, which few or none can make use of until it be metamorphosied into my pure and christaline form. Nay, in this transparent colour I have added thousands to his Majesty's forces, and for all these good offices I have done, I am doom'd to destruction.

And there is nothing hurts me more, than that of a temporary death, if ever I come again into existence. I am much afraid that many of my most intimate acquaintance will be gone forever to the place of oblivion, for want of that comfort which I usually gave to those who were my hourly companions.

It has been often said that I was the death of thousands of the liege subjects, but I can incontrovertibly prove that those who have forsaken, and given over taking me into their bosoms, have died very soon thereafter, whilst those who have continued by me, are living witnesses of the truth of what I aver, and I am certain before the end of January thousands will die with the greatest heaviness on their spirits for the want of ME to comfort them.

It is now proposed that all those who are possessed of Stills, will send them into the different barracks, now erected in the kingdom, in purpose that their masters may not be obliged to pay rent for useless utensils, and to gather all the lick sticks in the island to watch them; and as they will be out of employment, and for fear of them getting a bad habit of idleness, it will be requisite they undergo the exercise of their duty, in case they forget how to perform it when they are again set agoing. And besides this it will be another advantage, as they will defend the barracks, while our brave soldiers are keeping the French from landing on our Coasts; and if this employment shall be found to be too little for them to distill a little now and then of a superior strength, in order to manufacture powder with it, to shoot at the French if they shall attempt a landing, and if they should dare to land, these idle gentry will be ready to destroy whatever may remain, for fear of these banditti getting possession of it, as the Carmagnols are said to fight best when they have got drunk.

RIGHT An anonymous comic broadside against a government proposal to ban whisky making for six months in 1795.

They were often caught, no doubt, with the contraband whisky in their possession. Then they were subjected to heavy fines besides the loss of their goods. But – daring, stout, active fellows – they often broke through the nets … I have seen a troop of thirty of them riding Indian file, and in broad day, through the streets of Brechin, after they had succeeded in disposing of their whisky, and, as they rode leisurely along, beating time with their formidable cudgels on the empty barrels to the great amusement of the public and mortification of the excisemen … Everybody, with few exceptions, drank what was in reality illicit whisky – far superior to that made under the eye of the Excise – lords and lairds, members of parliament and ministers of the Gospel, and everybody else.

ABOVE John Murdoch (1818–1903), former exciseman turned newspaper owner and campaigner for crofter's rights.

RIGHT Aeneas Coffey's prototype continuous still was first patented in Dublin in 1831. Coffey, the city's former chief excise officer, failed to persuade Irish distillers to adopt his invention. He found a much more receptive audience in Scotland.

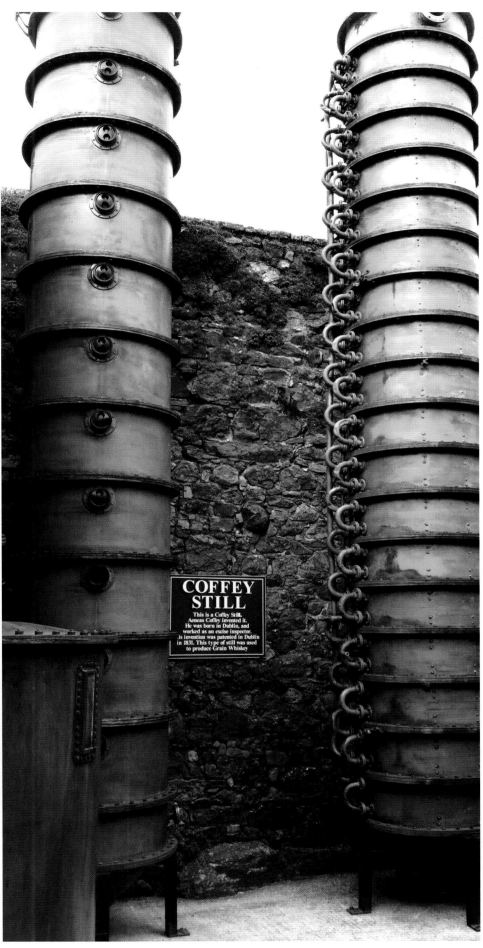

COFFEY STILL

This is a Coffey Still. Aeneas Coffey invented it. He was born in Dublin, and worked as an excise inspector. His invention was patented in Dublin in 1831. This type of still was used to produce Grain Whisky

LEGISLATION AND ROYAL PATRONAGE

BY 1822 THERE WAS EVEN A NAME FOR ILLICIT SCOTCH. IT WAS CALLED GLENLIVET – A REGIONAL STYLE OF WHISKY DEMANDED BY THE KING HIMSELF WHEN HE DESCENDED ON SCOTLAND THAT YEAR.

George IV's visit, masterminded by that bestselling author and consummate PR man, Walter Scott, was a big deal. It was the first time a reigning monarch had set foot north of the border since 1650. As for the whisky, it could have come from over 200 illicit stills said to be operating in this remote corner of Upper Speyside.

Despite enjoying royal patronage, the tide of opinion was beginning to turn against illicit whisky, at least among the landowners who were faced with tougher fines if their tenants were caught operating an unlicensed still. There was also a growing fear of anarchy if people so routinely flouted the law. Yet much more important in persuading illicit whisky makers to come in from the cold was the relaxation of the rules and a lowering of the fees. By halving the duty on spirit, and setting the licence at a modest £10, the Excise Act of 1823 became the midwife to the modern whisky industry.

The trickle of distillers who had previously been taking out licences turned into a spate that year as dozens followed suit. Not that every former smuggler decided to give up, and there were tales of distilleries like Lochnagar on Deeside being torched, and of distillers being attacked. Glenlivet's founder, George Smith – the first man to take out a licence in the glen – was confronted by a smuggling gang at an inn near Glenshee. According to legend, the ringleader burst into his room and threatened to disembowel him on the spot. Quick as a flash, Smith whipped out a pair of pistols from under the bed sheets, and held one to the man's head and fired the other up the chimney with a deafening blast.

Within five years of the Act, whisky production had trebled to an estimated 10 million gallons, while Campbeltown in deepest Argyll witnessed the industry's first boom with no fewer than 27 distilleries built between 1823 and 1837. Of course all of them were malt distilleries relying on old-fashioned pot stills which, then as now, had to be filled and emptied with each batch. Having done this with the wash still, you have to repeat the process with the spirit still to achieve the double distillation you need for Scotch.

A Thousand Warm receptions in the North

TOP King George IV's "Northern excursion" of 1822, the first time a reigning monarch had visited Scotland since 1650, and the tartan fest that ensued, inspired much satire. It was noted the King, dubbed "the portly Hanoverian", wore flesh-coloured tights beneath his kilt to conceal his gouty legs.

ABOVE Andrew Usher was the great pioneering Scotch whisky blender in Edinburgh whose OVG, or Old Vatted Glenlivet, was one of the first commercial blends ever produced. OVG was followed by the successful Usher's Green stripe.

BELOW For the princely sum of £4-14/6 (four pounds, 14 shillings and six pence) George Smith is granted a licence to make whisky at his distillery at Upper Drummin in the Parish of Glenlivet in 1849

RIGHT Just 15 years later, in 1864, George Smith's licence to make whisky at Drummin had more than doubled to £10-10/0 (ten pounds and ten shillings).

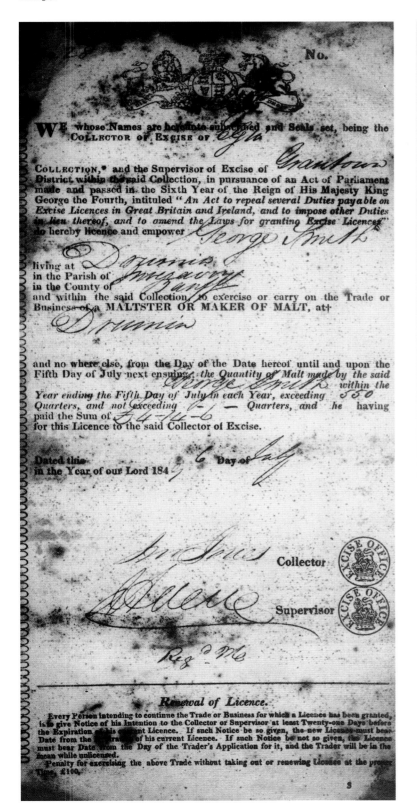

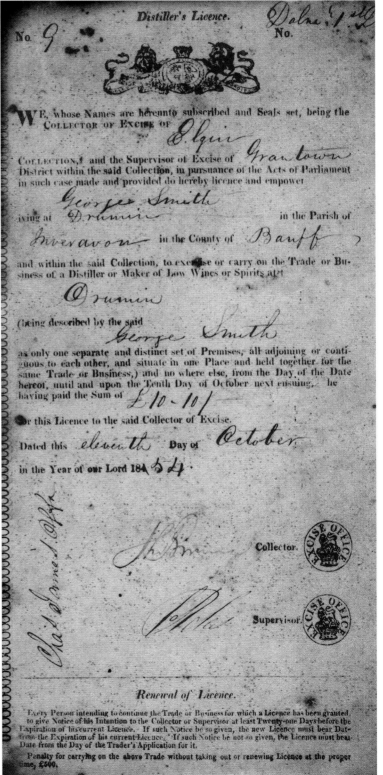

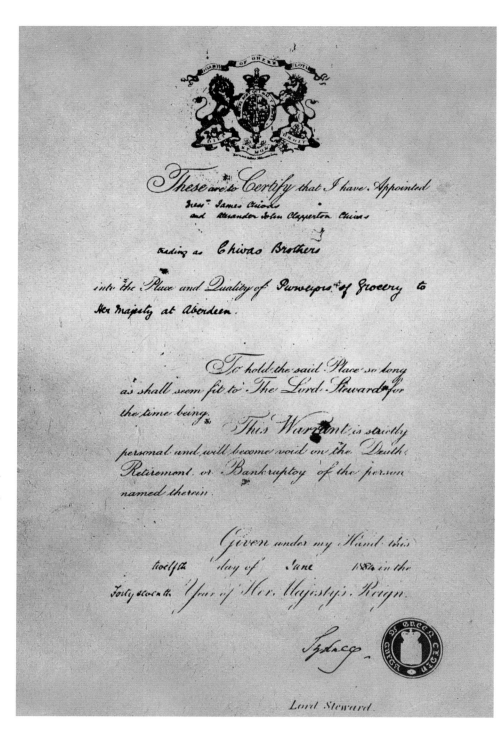

ABOVE What more did a captain in the Royal Navy need when at sea than a case of Andrew Usher's pioneering brand of Old Vatted Glenlivet?

LEFT Chivas Brothers' Royal Warrant as "Purveyors of Grocery to Her Majesty at Aberdeen" dated 12 June 1884.

SCOTCH BLENDS IN

Once there was grain and malt whisky to marry together, blended Scotch was an accident waiting to happen. However the early blenders stuck to mixing malts for a few decades yet, which gives the lie to a fair number of famous brands. Johnnie Walker may still be going strong, but it wasn't born in 1820. The father of blended whisky is said to be Andrew Usher, whose family-owned drinks business in Edinburgh happened to be agents for Glenlivet on Speyside. Usher began mixing the malts to produce Old Vatted

Glenlivet – known as OVG, and once the Spirits Act of 1860 allowed people to blend whiskies from different distilleries before duty was paid, he began adding grain whisky. The result was smoother, more rounded and cheaper to produce. In a few years he released the first true commercial blended Scotch – Usher's Green Stripe, which was soon flattered by imitation. Many of the early blends were cooked up by grocers like John Walker & Sons of Kilmarnock and Chivas Brothers in Aberdeen.

For all the romance of Highland whisky, with its

THE CONTINUOUS STILL

For a Scotsman in a hurry like Robert Stein, the plodding production of pot stills was completely out of step with the industrial revolution. Distilling's holy grail would be a still that could convert the wash into spirit in a continuous flow, and various prototypes were tested out by distillers on the Continent and in Ireland. Stein produced his "patent still" in 1828 and installed it at Cameronbridge distillery in Fife. The wash was heated and then sprayed into various chambers in a column separated by cloths. It certainly produced spirit, though how good it was is unclear. Despite Stein's best efforts, no other distiller was tempted to buy a patent still.

One man who did see the potential was Aeneas Coffey, who had retired from running Ireland's Excise to do a spot of distilling by himself in Dublin. This ultimate gamekeeper turned poacher gave the world the Coffey still in 1830, and after a few modifications involving copper plates within the metal columns, it became the standard continuous still. The history of whisky could have been very different had the Irish distillers not turned their noses up at his invention, causing Coffey to move to London in 1840. By then his stills were starting to appear in Scotland's new grain distilleries in the Lowlands. Before long they were pumping out a much blander, smoother spirit at up to 85 per cent alcohol by volume. By the mid-nineteenth century they were producing more alcohol than pot stills in Scotland and England, though not in Ireland.

reputation was badly dented, and Scotch seized its opportunity with both hands to present a credible alternative. Society magazines were blitzed with adverts featuring upper-crust types drinking whisky and soda in their London clubs. There were also frequent references to Highlanders, though copywriters appeared confused as to whether to portray them as noble warriors or comic drunks.

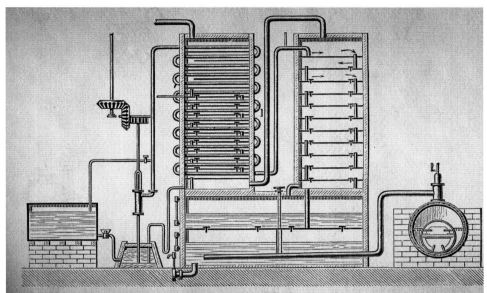

slow pot stills bubbling away in remote glens, it was the big city blenders who cajoled the malt distillers to up their game and produce a consistent, quality spirit. The blends they produced had to compete with popular, triple-distilled Irish whiskies, and convince the English bourgeoisie that Scotch had a place in their drinks cupboard. What was perceived as a crude, outdoor spirit, suitable for the grouse moor or river bank, craved the same social acceptance as brandy and soda.

Help was at hand from an unlikely source. A microscopic aphid called phylloxera with an insatiable appetite for vine roots was first spotted in France in 1863. Before long it was munching its way through swathes of vineyards, including those of Cognac. As prices soared, unscrupulous merchants began passing off cheaper brandies, before faking the spirit altogether. Cognac's

TOP An early diagram of a continuous still showing the two columns. The wash enters the rectifier on the right where the perforated copper plates strip out the heavier compounds and is then vaporized in the second column, or analyser, on the left.

ABOVE When George Smith first licensed Glenlivet in 1824, illicit distillers in the glen threatened to burn it to the ground with him in the middle. For his protection the Laird of Aberlour gave him this fine pair of hair-trigger revolvers that he kept with him at all times. They are now kept at the Glenlivet visitor centre.

THE WHISKY BARONS

JOHN DEWAR AND HIS YOUNGER BROTHER, TOMMY DEWAR, TURNED A LOCAL WHISKY BUSINESS IN PERTH INTO A GLOBAL GIANT ON THE BACK OF DEWAR'S WHITE LABEL.

The blend, now owned by Bacardi, sells around three million cases worldwide and still claims to be the most popular Scotch whisky in America. Back in 1880, when the Dewar brothers inherited the firm from their father, annual profits were a modest £1,231. While John Dewar looked after things in Scotland, Tommy was dispatched "to wake up the south" in 1885. He arrived in London aged 21 to discover one of his leads was dead and the other bankrupt.

In 1892 he set off from Liverpool aboard the *City of Paris* to conquer the world. He returned two years later, having visited 26 countries and appointed 32 agents, and though the venture cost a staggering sum no one minded back at company HQ. Orders were flooding in from Canada and the States. A second sales trip took him round South America and as far as New Zealand spreading the gospel of Dewar's White Label.

Tommy Dewar understood the power of advertising better than anyone in the whisky industry, and in 1895 launched "the whisky of his forefathers" – a campaign that ran for almost 40 years. It featured a slightly absurd creation – half Scot, half English gent – who sits nursing a dram while his ancestors stretch out of their portraits behind him to grab the bottle. There was even a filmed version, believed to be the first of its kind, which was shown on a rooftop screen in New York. Meanwhile Londoners gasped at a 200-foot illuminated Scotsman beside the Thames next to the firm's bottling hall, whose kilt and beard appeared to sway in the wind as his arm repeatedly raised a glass of Dewar's.

BELOW LEFT Tommy Dewar, the quintessential "Scotsman on the make", launched the Dewar's White Label brand and helped it become one of the world's biggest-selling blends. He was also an MP, then member of the House of Lords, and died a multi-millionaire.

BELOW Sir James Buchanan, Dewar's arch-rival and another natural-born salesman, launched the Buchanan's blend and Black & White. Eventually the two companies merged to form Buchanan Dewar Ltd, while Buchanan himself went on to become Lord Woolavington.

In 1895 Tommy Dewar became the third owner of a motor car in Britain, and before long was a fully-fledged member of the Establishment, with invitations to shooting parties featuring Edward VII. Like his brother he entered politics, becoming a Conservative MP in the unlikely constituency of London's Tower Hamlets until swept aside by the Liberals. In 1915 it was decided to merge John Dewar & Sons with arch-rival Buchanan's, which together were soon part of the Distillers Company (DCL). Both brothers became barons and died in the winter of 1929, each leaving an estate worth £5 million – or £270 million in today's money.

Peter Mackie, the father of White Horse, was "one third genius, one third megalomaniac and one third eccentric", claimed Sir Robert Bruce Lockhart, the diplomat, writer and secret agent. Mackie was born in 1855 and at 23 went to work for his uncle's whisky business in Glasgow, who were agents for Lagavulin and Laphroaig. It was on Islay that Mackie cut his teeth in the whisky trade and learned to love the island's whiskies, particularly Lagavulin. Of all the whisky barons, he was the most attached to malt whisky, though his fortune came from a blend.

Named after Edinburgh's White Horse Inn, it was launched in the UK in 1901 as "a brand of the highest age and quality, second to nothing that has ever been offered the public". The public appeared unimpressed and Mackie despaired of their ignorance. "If only they would ask for the right brand!" he cried, until eventually conceding that White Horse needed some promotion. Between 1902 and 1914, £90,000 was spent on advertising, causing sales to jump from 700 to 70,000 cases a year. As a dyed-in-the-wool Tory, he loathed the Liberal Chancellor Lloyd George, who raised the duty on spirits by a third in his 1909 budget.

As the debate over the demon drink raged, Mackie believed the answer lay in maturation. Years in oak casks not only mellowed the whisky, but mellowed the drinker too, he claimed. "Experience teaches us that the riotous and obstreperous conduct of drunks come from the young, fiery spirit which is sold. While men who may over-indulge in old matured whisky become sleepy and stupid, but not in a fighting mood." It was not until 1916, however, that the minimum three-year maturation for Scotch whisky became law.

By the outbreak of war exports had increased five-fold to 190,000 cases on 1900. There were other blends including the deluxe, 18-year-old *Logan's*

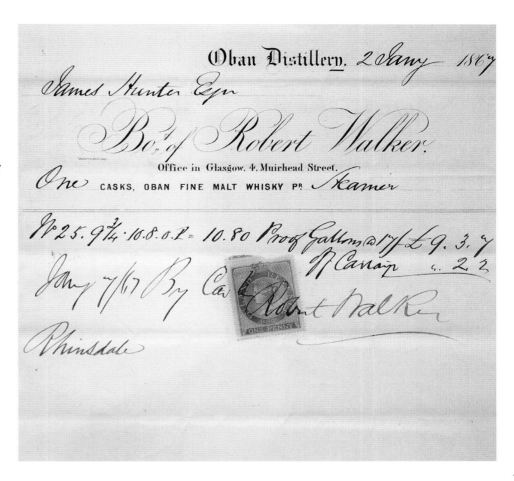

ABOVE An invoice from 1867 for a 10.80-gallon cask of malt whisky from Oban distillery £9-3/7.

BELOW An early label for Peter Mackie's famous brand launched in 1901. It was blended Scotch despite calling itself a "liqueur", and note the reference to "great age" as Mackie was a great believer in well-matured whisky.

Perfection, but the star was always White Horse with its heart of Lagavulin. On Islay, Mackie fell out with the Johnstones who owned Laphroaig. After a court case to end the agency, he ordered the distillery's water supply to be choked off. After being back in the dock, he built within the grounds of Lagavulin the Malt Mill distillery, in which he aimed and failed to produce a Laphroaig-like whisky. Mackie died in 1924 with his firm still independent. Three years later it was swallowed by DCL.

PLEASING THE PALATE

With his black silk top hat, monocle and auburn moustache, James Buchanan was the quintessential whisky baron who rode the late Victorian whisky boom with panache. He seemed to embody the smooth sophistication that blended Scotch aspired to, in contrast to the more earthy charms of malt whisky. The latter was seen as a raw Highland spirit that gentlemen could indulge in when out stalking or flogging Scotland's salmon rivers, but not indoors.

Buchanan was born in Brockville, Ontario in 1849, but his family soon returned to Scotland. He joined his brother, a grain merchant in Glasgow, and via grain slipped into the whisky trade to become the London agent for Charles Mackinlay & Co. at the age of 30. Five years later, with the backing of Glasgow blenders WP Lowrie who supplied the raw material, he created the Buchanan blend. "What I made up my mind to do," he later wrote, "was to find a blend sufficiently light and old to please the palate of the user."

He felt the heavy, well-peated flavours of Scottish malts would never appeal over the smoother, triple-distilled taste of Irish whiskey. By 1885 the first bottles of Buchanan's blend were being sold as "Fine old Scotch whiskies" and "Suitable either for Grog or Toddy". With its white label on a dark bottle, it became known as Black & White whisky – the name it eventually adopted as a brand.

Buchanan was a natural-born salesman who managed to get his whisky into the House of Commons, where he had become "sole supplier" by 1888, and before long had secured a royal warrant from Queen Victoria and Edward, Prince of Wales. He took over the Black Swan distillery in Holborn and rebuilt it into a Scottish Baronial headquarters for his business, complete with crenulations and turrets. In 1903 James Buchanan & Co. became a limited company.

To promote the whisky he would ride across town accompanied by a liveried footman in his red-wheeled buggy pulled by a black pony. By 1907 Buchanan's was the top-selling blend in Britain, and two years later he began proposing a merger with his biggest rivals. This eventually became Buchanan Dewar Ltd in 1919, which merged with John Walker & Sons into the Distillers Company in 1925. By then James Buchanan had become Baron Woolavington, with an estate and racehorse stud in Sussex, and properties in Kenya and Argentina. He died in 1935 leaving an estate valued at £7 million.

BELOW An original drawing of Johnnie Walker's famous striding man from 1908 by the cartoonist and graphic artist, Tom Browne. Note how is walking right to left. Since 2000 he has always been striding forwards.

TOM BROWNE

THE STRIDING MAN

The world's bestselling Scotch whisky rejoices under the strapline "Born 1820 – still going strong". In truth it is one of those myths that, through endless repetition, has morphed into fact. That may have been when *Johnnie Walker* opened his grocery shop in Kilmarnock, aged 15, but the whiskies came later.

Today's brand owners, Diageo, claim that he did blend malt whiskies in his shop, having learned the skill from blending tea, though there is a slight dearth of evidence. What is known is that it was not until after his death in 1857 that his son Alexander Walker produced Walker's Old Highland whisky, the first commercially available blend. He introduced the famous square bottle and slanting label, though it was the next generation, George and Alexander Walker, together with the firm's newly appointed MD, James Stevenson, who really created the brand. They registered Johnnie Walker Red and Black Label in 1909, together with a short-lived White Label that was withdrawn when Dewar's complained.

The "striding man" logo was sketched on a napkin over lunch by the commercial artist Tom Browne in 1908. With his red tailcoat, top hat and monocle he was definitely more lion tamer than Scottish grocer. Indeed had he been spotted on the streets of Kilmarnock in 1820, people would have assumed the circus was in town. Nevertheless, as a brand icon he certainly stood out in the sea of tartan that dominated whisky marketing at the time. By 1920 Johnnie Walker whisky had marched into 120 foreign markets before Coca-Cola had crossed the Atlantic.

By strange coincidence Johnnie Walker's great rival *Chivas Regal* was also registered in 1909, and not quite the 1801 that was claimed on the label. It was the flagship blend of the Chivas Brothers grocery store in Aberdeen. It was the city's answer to London's Fortnum & Mason: a grand emporium that stocked everything from "curious brandies" to "sperm candles" – just two of the items mentioned in early adverts. The store secured a royal warrant from Queen Victoria in 1843, two years before she bought Balmoral. Before long the brothers were blending whiskies in the basement, reserving the oldest and best malts for Chivas Regal, whose range stretched to a 25-year-old by 1915.

It was "regal" more in aspiration than anything, and *Sam Bronfman* was able to buy Chivas Brothers

BELOW LEFT Sir Alexander Walker, grandson of the original Johnnie Walker, took over the business in 1889 with his brother George. He was responsible for blending and created Red Label and later Johnnie Walker Swing.

BELOW Johnnie Walker's iconic striding man dates from 1908 and is said to enjoy the same brand recognition as Coca-Cola. The logo is now always shown left to right, striding forward. In the past Johnnie Walker was often portrayed walking in the other direction.

Johnnie Walker ®

FAR LEFT For the man who has everything – a US print advert for Chivas Regal from 1985.

LEFT Chivas Brothers was the Fortnum & Mason of Aberdeen. It stocked everything from "curious brandies" to "sperm candles", plus innumerable wines and spirits, especially whisky as per this 1890 price list.

BELOW Founded in 1786, Strathisla in Keith on Speyside is one of the oldest distilleries in Scotland, and undoubtedly one of the most handsome. It now belongs to Chivas Brothers – the Scotch whisky division of the French group Pernod Ricard.

for £85,000 in 1949. The grandeur of the name and certainly the royal warrant appealed to Bronfman, the boss of Seagram's, who in later years was said to crave a knighthood that never came. "It was Mr Sam's intention to make Chivas Regal the greatest name in Scotch whisky," a colleague later recalled. "This was not just a man marketing a new product – it was an artist producing his chef d'oeuvre." By the time the 1960s had got going, Seagram's had turned Chivas Regal 12-year-old into an almost unstoppable force.

CUTTY SARK

If Sam Bronfman was the swashbuckling liquor baron born out of Prohibition, *Francis Berry* appeared to be his polar opposite. In 1907 he and his first cousin Walter took over Berry Brothers – the most venerable wine merchants in London, if not the world. With roots stretching back to 1698, its emporium in St James became a stopping off point between coffee shops, gambling clubs and assembly rooms for London Society. By the end of the nineteenth century Berry's were selling whisky "either Scotch or Irish" at £1.16s. a case (£160 in today's money) alongside "ordinary sherry",

"superior sherry" and "second quality port".

Nothing as brash as a brand name was mentioned, though eventually that changed and in 1923 the firm launched a blend of whisky named after the famous Clyde-built clipper – the *Cutty Sark*. It was aimed at the American market, then officially "dry" during Prohibition, and was pale in colour with no added caramel like cognac – Francis Berry's preferred spirit. The brand and the label design were cooked up over lunch above the shop, and before long Cutty Sark whisky was being shipped to Nassau – the end of the British distribution chain to the US. From there it was bootlegged into America by men like Captain Bill McCoy. While the country's "speakeasies" and drinking dens were awash with fake whiskies sometimes cut with lethal wood alcohol, this genuine Scotch was the real McCoy. Francis Berry died just three years after the repeal of Prohibition in 1933, but he had laid the foundations for a great brand. By the mid-1970s Cutty Sark had become one of the most popular blends in the States, and went on to enjoy similar success in Spain. Life has become tougher since for the Edrington Group who now own the brand.

BOTTOM LEFT An imperious Sam Bronfman, with son and heir, Edgar Bronfman waiting at his shoulder, circa 1966.

BELOW Named after a famous Clyde-built clipper that was in turn named after the witch in Burns's poem "Tam o' Shanter", Cutty Sark the blended Scotch whisky was born in 1923 and gained a strong following in the USA during Prohibition.

CUTTY SARK
SCOTCH WHISKY

100% SCOTCH WHISKIES
86 PROOF

From Scotland's Best Distilleries

THE BUCKINGHAM CORPORATION · NEW YORK, N.Y.

WHISKY AND THE BRITISH EMPIRE

WITH COGNAC IN CRISIS, DISTILLERIES IN SCOTLAND AND IRELAND BEGAN TO REALIZE THE WORLD WAS UP FOR GRABS, STARTING WITH ENGLAND. FOR MOST OF THE VICTORIAN WHISKY BOOM THE SMART MONEY WAS ON THE IRISH.

When the Distillers Company (DCL) built Dublin's Phoenix Park distillery in 1878, it claimed that demand for Irish "whiskey" was five times greater than for Scotch. With its smooth, pot still taste, it was considered superior to the rougher, often un-aged blends coming from Scotland. Not that the Scots were above blurring the lines between the two styles. The giant Caledonian distillery, one of the biggest in Scotland, was one of several supplying what it called "the variety known as Irish". Despite coming from a five-acre site in Edinburgh, the whisky was declared to be "precisely similar to that which is made in Dublin".

Unlike the big urban distillers of Ireland, Scottish blenders had to source their malts from a wider area. Having relied principally on those in Campbeltown, the Lowlands and the Central Highlands, they began to look north. Meanwhile the railways, which had already stretched upwards to Aberdeen and Inverness, began to branch out into Speyside. For all the romantic imagery of smugglers and illicit whisky, it was probably the advent of the Strathspey railway in 1863 that did more to create the biggest epicentre of malt whisky production in Scotland. Distilleries popped up beside the track like homesteads in the American Midwest. Typically they would connect to the main line via a siding and would have their own tank engine, or pug, to transport the sacks of grain and coal in and the newly filled barrels of whisky out.

"The future of the wine trade is whisky," declared the *Wine Trade Review* in 1886, and the orderly spread of distilleries down the Spey valley turned into a stampede. A staggering 33 distilleries were built in Scotland in the last decade of the nineteenth century, two-thirds of them in this one region. There was plentiful East Coast barley nearby, no shortage of water or fuel, an established skilled workforce, easy money from banks and private investors and a seemingly insatiable demand from the blenders. What could possibly go wrong? Step forward one Robert Patterson Pattison and his brother Walter Gilchrist Gray Pattison.

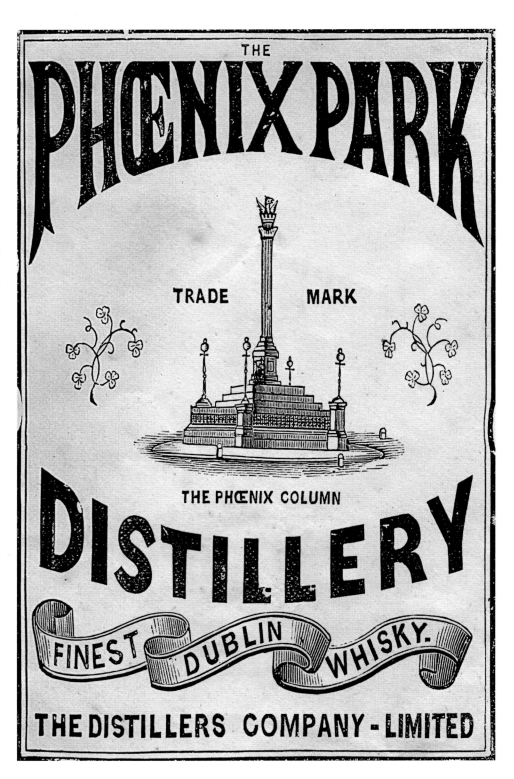

THE PHŒNIX PARK

THE PHŒNIX COLUMN

DISTILLERY

FINEST DUBLIN WHISKY.

THE DISTILLERS COMPANY - LIMITED

TRADE MARK

THE PATTISON CRASH

"The booming of the cannon is nothing to the booming of Pattison's whisky," thundered an advertisement featuring the massed ranks of a Highland artillery regiment. It was typical hubris from the Pattison brothers of Leith, who left the humdrum world of dairy wholesaling to leap into bed with this sexy new spirit. They set up as blenders in 1887 and floated the company on the London Stock Exchange two years later. It was said that the offer was six times oversubscribed.

They soon had a lavish, marbled HQ in Leith and a giant warehouse, and they hired 150 salesmen – more than their much larger rival, DCL. They were also spending an unprecedented £60,000 on advertising by 1898 – around £5 million in today's money. As well as adverts full of imperial bombast, the firm recruited 500 African grey parrots and taught them to squawk

OPPOSITE The late Victorian whisky boom was a two-horse race between the Scots and the Irish, and the smart money was on the Irish. In 1878 the Distillers Co. built the Phoenix Park distillery in Dublin and claimed the country's whisky was five times greater than Scotch.

LEFT A suitably bombastic advert from the Pattison brothers of Leith whose blend became one of the biggest spirits brands in the country before the company crashed in spectacular fashion in 1899, almost bringing the entire whisky industry down with it.

in endless repetition, "Buy Pattison's whisky!" – or so it was claimed.

Financed by debt and engaged in some creative accounting, the Pattison brothers, who were by now as rich as Croesus, could only keep it up so long as Scotch whisky itself kept growing. At the start of the 1890s there was just under two million gallons of malt whisky in Scotland's warehouses. By 1898 the amount had soared to over 13 million, and in December the Clydesdale Bank pulled the plug on Pattison's. Its crash brought down nine other companies in its wake and bankrupted scores of small suppliers. Three years later the two brothers were sent down for 9–18 months for fraud and embezzlement. Yet what had happened was a classic speculative bubble that would have burst with or without the Pattisons.

HANGOVER AND IDENTITY CRISIS

The Scotch whisky industry entered the twentieth century awash with stock and gripped by the worst hangover in its history. The Pattison affair left a deep impression on William Ross, the newly appointed MD of the Distillers Company, who vowed to bring supply and demand closer together and ensure there would be no repetition of the reckless speculation that had caused the crash. Ailing distilleries and blenders were bought up and, if necessary, closed down. Within two decades all the top-selling blends – Johnnie Walker, Dewar's, White Horse and Buchanan's – were under the DCL umbrella.

Meanwhile there was the question of whisky's identity. What exactly was Scotch? Should it be wholly or mainly malt whisky, or did it not matter? Did it even need to come from Scotland? Having stamped out some "adulterated brandy" in 1905, Islington Council in London turned on some so-called "Fine Old Scotch". This led to a Royal Commission in 1908 where both sides – the Highland malt mafia and the grain whisky barons like DCL, put their case. Interestingly, had the malt distillers backed a proposal from Alexander Walker for a 50 per cent minimum malt content in blends, the history of Scotch would have been very different. Sir Peter Mackie, the father of White Horse and the whisky baron most closely linked to malt

BELOW LEFT DCL spent the interwar years buying up its rivals and closing down surplus distilleries to emerge as the big white whale of the whisky trade.

BELOW David Lloyd George, Britain's Chancellor of the Exchequer (1908–15) and then wartime Prime Minister, was a thorn in the side of the whisky industry. While he never succeeded in his crusade to "abolish thirst", he did clobber the trade with tax.

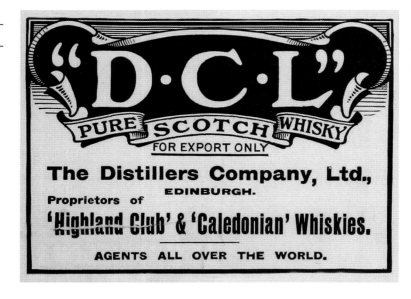

whisky, was able to concede that the blenders may have had the industry's best interests at heart. As he put it later: "Had the trade in whisky been confined to malt, unmellowed by grain spirit, the trade would not be a tenth of what it is today."

In the end the Commission failed to resolve anything. Yet by 1909 a bigger threat loomed in the shape of Lloyd George's budget, which pushed the price of a standard blend to over half a crown (2s.6d.). Many in the industry saw it as a death knell, and part of the Liberal chancellor's crusade to "abolish thirst". Temperance had a long history, with the first temperance society in Scotland founded in 1829, and for a century excise duty had made up 30–40 per cent of government revenue – far more than income tax.

Yet there had never been a moral dimension to excise duty until now. The only good news for the whisky industry was the growth of exports to 7.5 million proof gallons by 1909, Australia being the biggest consumer, followed by the US, Canada and South Africa.

LEFT Scotch whisky oiled the wheels of the British Empire which proved to be a lucrative captive market.

THE GREAT WAR AND PROHIBITION

WITHIN A YEAR OF THE OUTBREAK OF THE FIRST WORLD WAR IN 1914, LLOYD GEORGE WAS TELLING THE NATION THERE WAS A MORE DAMNING THREAT THAN GERMAN U-BOATS. "WE ARE FIGHTING GERMANY, AUSTRIA AND DRINK; AND AS FAR AS I CAN SEE THE GREATEST OF THESE DEADLY FOES IS DRINK."

The forces ranged against alcohol had become increasingly politicized. In 1901 the Scottish Prohibition Party was co-founded by Edwin Scrymgeour, who became a Dundee councillor and eventually the city's MP in 1922. After that election, in which he defeated none other than Winston Churchill, he held the seat as the only Prohibitionist MP in Parliament until 1931.

Back in 1914 at the outbreak of the First World War, there was a clamour to ban distilling altogether. The industry, led by the redoubtable William Ross, head of DCL, retaliated by arguing that distilling was essential for the war effort. It provided yeast for baking bread, dope for waterproofing aeroplane wings, and spirit for use in anaesthetics and for making high explosives.

BELOW New York speakeasy in 1933 in the dying days of Prohibition.

Though malt distilling pretty much ceased, the grain distilleries kept going, allowing Dewar's to supply some three million bottles of its White Label blend to the Army and Navy catering corps. Meanwhile two issues concerning whisky were resolved during the war. By 1917, the minimum strength had been set at 40 per cent alcohol by volume (80 proof) and the spirit had to be aged in oak casks for a minimum of three years before it could be called Scotch whisky.

The price of a bottle of Scotch had been fixed at 12 shillings. After the war this was raised by half a shilling, while the duty was doubled and then raised again, squeezing the big blenders in the process. The resentment of whisky drinkers for having to pay 12s.6d. was given vent in a popular music hall refrain: "How can a fella be happy – when happiness costs such a lot?" And yet at least whisky was still legal on this side of the Atlantic.

BOOTLEGGERS AND SPEAKEASIES

On the pretext of ensuring that cereals and fruit were kept solely for the food chain, alcohol production was banned in America when the country entered the First World War in 1917. By December of that year the Anti-Saloon League led by the ruthless political lobbyist, Wayne Wheeler, helped to ram a prohibition amendment through Congress. It was eventually passed in January 1919 and became law a year later.

In the months before, drinks like Scotch whisky flooded in, and those with means, including plenty of congressmen, stockpiled whatever they could for the dry years ahead. Within hours of Prohibition

BELOW Just as distillers kept track of what was produced at a distillery, so they also logged details of the grain supplied to them. These pages from the barley book of Cardhu Distillery show some of their suppliers during 1908–09.

there was a foretaste of things to come when an armed gang seized a lorry carrying medicinal alcohol in Chicago.

Surgical spirit was allowed, as was industrial alcohol and the use of alcohol for sacramental purposes. All three became widely exploited loopholes over the next 13 years. What was left of the trade simply disappeared underground as bars became "speakeasies", and legitimate spirits morphed into moonshine or "bathtub gin". By 1925 estimated consumption had fallen by as much as 60 per cent of its pre-Prohibition level, but thereafter it began to rise. It did so because in the public mind the case for Prohibition had never really been won, and because it went against human nature. The American lyricist, Vaughan Miller, put it succinctly:

There ain't going to be no more whiskey
There ain't going to be no more gin
There ain't going to be no more highballs to put
the whiskey in
There ain't going to be no more cigarettes to make folks
pale and thin
But you can't take away that tendency to sin, sin, sin.

While the Americans may have drunk less, they drank proportionately more spirits, not least because spirits offered the bootleggers better margins than beer or wine. In cities like New York, there was a certain thrill in slipping into an illicit drinking den where many new cocktails were spawned to mask the rough moonshine underneath – by the late 1920s America was the world's biggest importer of cocktail shakers. Eighty years later, a rash of retro "speakeasy" bars began popping up to re-create that mix of glamour and subterfuge of the Prohibition era.

IN SEARCH OF LIQUOR

Back in Scotland it was soon clear that American demand for whisky had not been choked off. Instead it was flooding over the world's longest international border from Canada, and from what became known as Rum Row. This was the line just beyond US territorial waters where trade could be done between the middlemen and the actual smugglers. Like an auction house with dubious ethics, the trick for Scotch whisky distillers was to keep the "fence" at a distance.

Berry Brothers & Rudd, a pillar of the establishment among London wine merchants, was heavily involved in the trade through Cutty Sark – the

BELOW LEFT Whisky in wartime – a break from the trenches.

BELOW Sam Bronfman, the Canadian liquor baron who made a fortune from bootlegging during Prohibition and went on to found the Seagram empire.

blend it created in 1923. That the firm was involved in spirits came to the attention of the notorious gangster Jack Diamond who, with his five quashed convictions for homicide, was not a typical Berry's customer. Known as "Legs" Diamond for his skill on the dance floor, he travelled to Europe in search of liquor. History is hazy over the precise details of his request for 300 cases of "gen-U-ine" Scotch whisky for cash in the early 1920s. No one really knows whether he came in person to the Berry Bros shop in St James's Street, but it would have been quite a scene.

While blends like Cutty Sark were coming in from Nassau, Sam Bronfman and his clan were extremely busy on the Canadian border. Having set up as the

Canada Pure Drug Co. in 1918, they secured the agency for Dewar's and established a string of so-called boozoriums along the Saskatchewan–North Dakota border. As well as legitimate blends like Dewar's, the Bronfmans offered cheaper alternatives like *Parker's Old Irish*, *Johnny Walker* and that "well-known" malt – *Glen Levitt*. The real cheap stuff was made in an oak-lined tank from distilled water, alcohol, sulphuric acid and a little caramel. The acid would eat into the wood to somehow replicate the ageing process. But unlike some of their rivals, the Bronfmans never used adulterated spirit or the embalming fluid sold by a Minneapolis undertaker for a dollar a gallon.

LEFT Britain's only Prohibitionist MP, Edwin Scrymgeour, who beat Winston Churchill in Dundee in the 1922 election and held the seat until 1931.

CHANGING TIMES

US PROHIBITION ENDED ON 5 DECEMBER 1933, HAVING COLLAPSED UNDER THE WEIGHT OF ITS UNINTENDED CONSEQUENCES. IT HAD CAUSED SIGNIFICANT UNEMPLOYMENT FROM BOTTLING LINES TO BREWERIES AND LIQUOR STORES, HAD DEPLETED STATE REVENUE OF DRINK TAX, AND HAD PASSED AN INDUSTRY WORTH US$3 BILLION INTO THE HANDS OF ORGANIZED CRIME.

The repeal of Prohibition was great news for the Scotch whisky industry, which had been suffering bleak times at home, where a cash-strapped government had ramped up excise duty. Sales were badly down anyway thanks to the Depression, and by the summer of 1933 there were only two malt distilleries in Scotland still operating– Glenlivet and Glen Grant.

The promised, pent-up demand from America took a while to come through because of initially high tariffs, but by 1939 the US was importing over 4.5 million gallons out of a total production of almost 38 million. By the outbreak of the Second World War the number of distilleries back in operation had climbed to 92, though that soon dwindled as supplies of imported grain grew scarcer. Whisky drinkers at home were hit by higher taxes to help the war effort, though this encouraged a vibrant black market to spring up. Meanwhile the government did what it could to encourage whisky exports, particularly to the States, to help Britain's balance of trade.

TRANSATLANTIC CONVOYS SET SAIL

Merchant ships would rendezvous in Loch Ewe between Skye and Ullapool, and then set off in convoy across the Atlantic. Among them, in February 1941, was the SS *Politician* which had been loaded with a quarter of a million bottles of Scotch. It ran aground near the tip of South Uist by the island of Eriskay, where the grateful locals helped themselves to precious bottles. The ending by shipwreck of a prolonged whisky drought was the inspiration for Compton Mackenzie's *Whisky Galore!*

Despite treacherous rocks and prowling U-boats, plenty of whisky did get through, although Scotland's distilleries had all shut by 1943 until restrictions on grain were lifted a year later. There were fears that the industry would be crippled beyond repair when the war ended, but it

had an ally in the Prime Minister. In April 1945, in a famous memo, Winston Churchill wrote: "On no account reduce the barley for whisky. This takes years to mature and is an invaluable export and dollar producer. Having regard to all our other

BELOW At 5.32pm, Eastern Standard Time, on 5 December 1933 Utah became the 36th State to ratify the 21st Amendment bringing an end to Prohibition and a near 14-year drought. Yet despite the headline many Americans were already back on the booze by then.

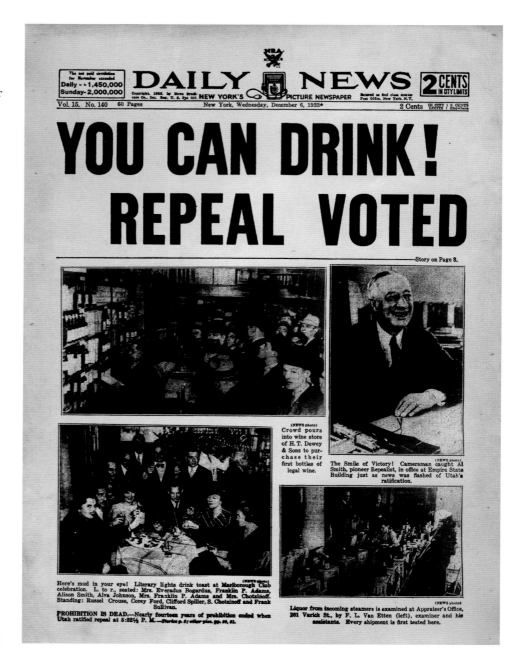

difficulties about export, it would be improvident not to preserve this characteristic British element of ascendancy." This was not something Lloyd George would have ever written. Churchill's favourite spirit was actually cognac, though most mornings he drank a very weak Johnnie Walker on ice – known within the family as a "Papa Cocktail". He considered the four essentials of life to be "hot baths, cold champagne, new peas and old brandy".

SEAGRAM'S LEADS THE WAY

In *The Making of Scotch Whisky*, John Hume and Michael Moss concluded: "By the end of the Second World War, the Scotch whisky industry had

endured forty-five years of adversity." Many firms had gone to the wall, or been bought up by the ever-expanding Distillers Company, which had been formed from the merger of the big three blending houses, and later swallowed up its two biggest rivals. Yet the company's big brands, notably Johnnie Walker, Dewar's and White Horse, were run like separate fiefdoms. Meanwhile the North Americans were now major players in the industry, led by Seagram's, who bought Chivas Brothers in 1949 for £85,000 – around £2.7 million today.

Britain's war-torn economy emerged blinking into the 1950s with a desperate need for foreign cash. Scotch whisky was a high-value commodity

ABOVE Based on a true story, Compton Mackenzie's famous novel became a box-office hit when the Ealing comedy *Whisky Galore* was released in 1949.

RIGHT Whether or not Laphroaig was being sold as a "medicinal spirit" in the United States during Prohibition, the brand was US trademarked in 1934.

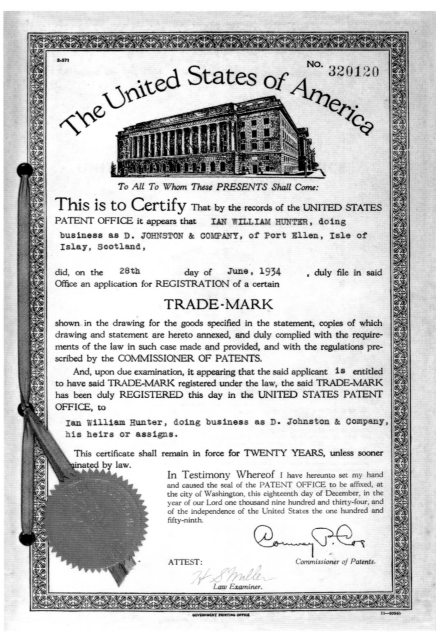

that could not be made anywhere else and thus fitted the bill perfectly. With rationing at home and a black market that allegedly accounted for one in three bottles drunk, there was every incentive to look abroad. Indeed the post-war Labour government only released barley to the distillers on the basis that at least two-thirds of production was shipped overseas.

THE SPIRIT OF THE AMERICAN DREAM

Scotch whisky was dispatched to all corners of the Commonwealth, to the old colonial outposts and far-flung emerging markets from Patagonia to Papua New Guinea. Yet nothing could rival the booming middle-class consumption in the US, particularly during the 1960s. By 1968 American consumers were drinking around 160 million bottles of Scotch a year, up almost three times since the start of the decade. Among the favoured brands

LEFT Glen Keith was one of the new post-war distilleries built by Seagram to provide malt whisky for its top-selling blends like Chivas Regal and 100 Pipers.

BELOW Production records for the Talisker distillery on Skye in a pre-computer age. Note the mash bill recorded in bushels of malt, and in gallons.

STATEMENT OF PRODUCE.

TALISKER DISTILLERY

Period No. 34 — Season 1956-1957 — Week Ending 4th MAY 1957

were Dewar's White Label, Cutty Sark and J&B Rare, while fighting it out among 12-year-old deluxe blends were Johnnie Walker Black Label and Chivas Regal.

"It was Mr Sam [Bronfman]'s intention to make Chivas Regal the greatest name in Scotch whisky. This was not just a man marketing a new product – it was an artist producing his chef d'oeuvre," a colleague wrote of the Seagram boss. In 1962 Chivas donned its glitzy metallic packaging, and enjoyed a new marketing campaign. It was a smooth blend – "No back bite. No gasp. No wince. No shudder". For US whisky drinkers it was almost the spirit of the American Dream.

NEW AND ONCE QUIET DISTILLERIES SPRING UP

In 1959 Seagram built Glen Keith, the first new distillery in Scotland since the late Victorian whisky boom; it was the starting gun for a new surge in production which, in the case of grain whisky, had more than doubled by 1966. This was the result of big new grain distilleries at Invergordon and Girvan. Before long malt whisky was catching up.

Everywhere disused distilleries were dragged out of retirement and the stills fired into life, while others like Glenturret and Caperdonich were rebuilt. Many added more stills, including Glenfarclas and Dalmore which were doubled, and five completely new distilleries were built, four from scratch and one – Deanston in Perthshire – converted from an old cotton mill. Of the new distilleries, the most striking was Tormore on Speyside. Constructed in 1960 of pale granite with massive arched windows and a chimney stack shaped like a whisky bottle, it symbolized the industry's post-war confidence like nothing else. Sadly the good times were not to last.

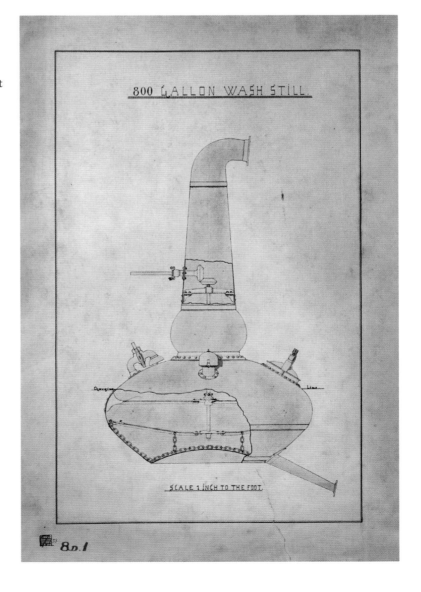

800 GALLON WASH STILL.

SCALE 1 INCH TO THE FOOT.

8.D.1

TOP A scale model of Tormore distillery kept at the Scotch Whisky Heritage Centre in Edinburgh. The Speyside distillery built in 1960 with massive arched windows and a chimney stack shaped like a whisky bottle symbolized the industry's post-war confidence.

RIGHT Design for an 800-gallon wash still, showing exterior and interior.

THE WHISKY LOCH AND THE RISE OF MALTS

THE PRODUCTION OF SCOTCH WHISKY CONTINUED TO EXPAND THROUGHOUT THE 1970S AS THOUGH THE SALES GRAPH WOULD CONTINUE ITS UPWARD TRAJECTORY AD INFINITUM.

Exports did keep growing until 1978, reaching the equivalent of almost 100 million bottles, but demand in what was by far the biggest market – the USA – had peaked a few years earlier. Many whisky firms had failed to recruit new drinkers, and their brands were fading into retirement like their loyal fans, while that hip, cosmopolitan spirit known as vodka was making waves on both sides of the Atlantic. In America a new generation simply didn't want to drink the same old J&B, Cutty or "Doo-ers" as their old man.

Back in Scotland, alarm bells were ringing on the bridge of the good ship whisky, with over a billion gallons of stock sitting in distillery warehouses by 1975. It was time to hit the brakes, but as with any super-tanker there's a big time lag between doing so and actually slowing down. Unlike vodka, which can be sold as soon as it is cold from the still, every drop of Scotch whisky has to spend at least three years in wood until it can be designated as such. To make things harder, there was not just one captain on the bridge but many, given all the industry bosses who each had their own sales forecasts.

In Britain the introduction of VAT in 1982, together with that year's duty increase, added £1.20 to the price of a standard bottle of Scotch. With the whisky loch full to the brim, DCL culled 11 of its 45 distilleries in May 1983, of which only Knockdhu and Benromach were later resuscitated. A year later the company closed another batch of distilleries, including four that never reopened. The fate of a "mothballed" distillery often depended on location. If it was out in the wilds, it might remain dormant for decades before resurrection when Scotch whisky's fortunes were on the rise again, while those in cities were soon sold off and redeveloped. Inverness lost all three of its distilleries at this time, including Glen Albyn whose bones lie buried beneath a shopping mall.

OPPOSITE Mackinlay's 1902 map of Scotland's distilleries. Those that are no longer with us include Stronachie, Bankier and Bo'Ness.

BELOW Port Ellen on Islay, one of nine DCL distilleries that closed for good in 1983, although the Port Ellen Maltings, which supplies the island's distilleries with most of their malt, is still going strong.

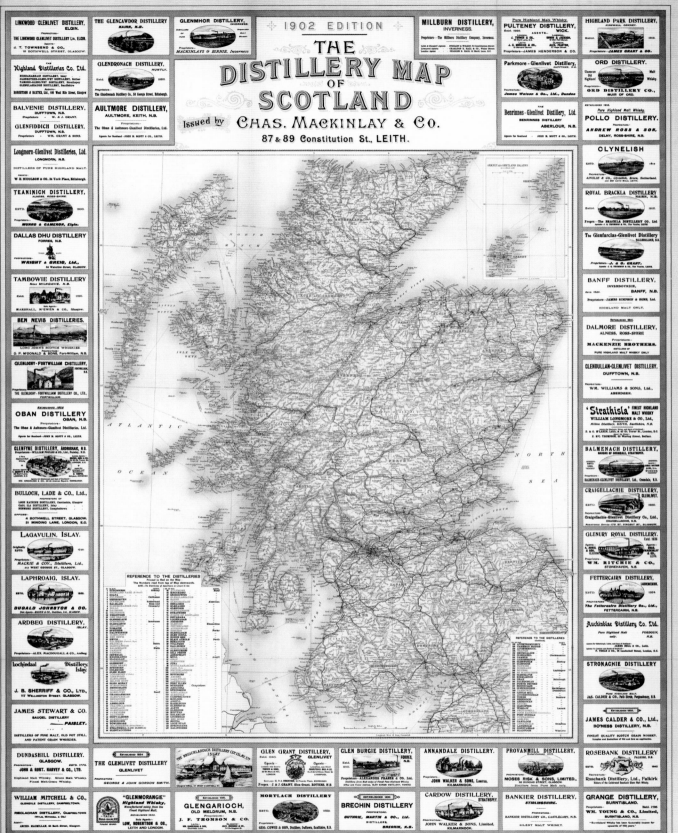

Scotch was losing out in the UK both to white spirits like Smirnoff and Bacardi and to wine, whose sales had trebled in a generation by the 1990s. The tax on wine was slashed by 20 per cent in 1984 to comply with EU rules, while spirits like whisky were hammered by successive chancellors. All this had an impact on the once mighty DCL, but many of its problems were self-inflicted. Having seen its share of the domestic whisky market collapse from 75 per cent in the early 1960s to just 16 per cent, it now found that the predators were at the gates. The Argyll Group, led by James Gulliver, made a hostile bid for the company in 1985. At £1.9 billion it was then the largest offer in UK history, but DCL turned to Guinness to be its saviour. In the end the beer giant triumphed with an offer of £2.7 billion and the combined group became United Distillers & Vintners, or UDV. The deal reeked of scandal, however, and Ernest Saunders, the boss of Guinness, was convicted of fraud and sent to prison. He was released after just 10 months suffering from acute senile dementia, from which he then made a "miraculous" recovery.

THE GREAT SINGLE MALT REVIVAL

Single malt whisky made in a copper pot still was the original Scotch, before the advent of blends following the invention of the continuous still in the 1820s. So completely did blends take over, that the taste of malt whisky virtually disappeared. It was obviously known to the distillery manager and his friends, and perhaps to some of the locals. Beyond Scotland, a small band of connoisseurs knew where to unearth bottles of Macallan, Talisker and the like, but that was about it.

By 1964 William Grant & Sons was having some success with its Glenfiddich five-year-old malt in Scotland, and decided it deserved a wider audience. It was relaunched as an eight-year-old pure malt in a patented, triangular dark bottle with a grand, silvery label not unlike Chivas Regal. Glenfiddich seeped southwards into England and then abroad, initially via duty-free, and by 1970 annual sales had reached 24,000 cases. The big whisky companies doubted whether single malts would ever catch on with consumers who had been taught, through endless adverts, to appreciate the smooth, mellow

BELOW LEFT Glen Grant five-year-old became a huge success in Italy, outselling all other whisky brands, whether blended or single malt. The Speyside distillery is now owned by the Italian spirits giant, Campari.

BELOW The distinctive stills at Glen Grant distillery on Speyside with their unique square-shaped reflux balls.

nature of blends. Distillers loved to boast how these were greater than the sum of their parts, and how they resembled an orchestra where the malts and the grain whiskies were the instruments. On their own, malts seemed too pungent, raw and full of flavour to ever seduce mainstream whisky drinkers – at least that was the view of many in the industry.

The independents like Macallan and Glenmorangie soon followed Glenfiddich's lead by laying down stock and releasing their own aged malts. Others joined in, yet even by 1980 single malts accounted for less than 1 per cent of all Scotch whisky. At the time the place where you were most likely to come across them was Italy. The country's regional importers would come over to Scotland and buy casks for bottling under the distillery name. The leading malt was Glen Grant five-year-old, whose sales had passed 200,000 cases by 1977, making it the country's biggest-selling whisky of all.

Finally the big white whale of the industry – UDV (the predecessor to Diageo) – decided in 1988 to release the Classic Malts range, based on the key whisky regions. Representing Islay and Skye were Lagavulin

and Talisker, along with Glenkinchie for the Lowlands, Oban for the West Coast, Dalwhinnie for the Highlands and Cragganmore for Speyside. They were picked as picturesque distilleries producing single malt. Judging by the size of Oban, for example, with its solitary pair of stills, no one foresaw how popular the range, and single malts in general, would become. They now account for a tenth of all the Scotch whisky drunk.

BELOW The Classic Malts stretched from Glenkinchie in the Lowlands to Talisker on the Isle of Skye, covering all the whisky regions bar Campbeltown.

BOTTOM Glenfiddich pioneered the modern era of single malt whisky when it launched its eight-year-old in the mid-1960s. Before long it was replaced with a 12-year-old to compete directly with deluxe blends like Chivas Regal and Johnnie Walker Black Label.

PART TWO

ON THE WHISKY TRAIL

ISLAY

OF ALL SCOTLAND'S WHISKY REGIONS, ISLAY HAS
BY FAR THE STRONGEST IDENTITY. BEING AN ISLAND
OBVIOUSLY PLAYS A BIG PART, BUT THERE IS ALSO ITS
FAMOUS SIGNATURE TUNE OF PEAT SMOKE EMBRACED
BY ALL OF ISLAY'S DISTILLERIES WITH THE EXCEPTION
OF BUNNAHABHAIN. THERE WAS NEVER A CONSCIOUS
DECISION TO PRODUCE PEATY WHISKIES; IT WAS
SIMPLY THAT PEAT WAS THE ONLY SOURCE OF FUEL
AVAILABLE ON THE ISLAND. PEOPLE HEATED THEIR
CROFTS WITH A CENTRAL FIRE FROM WHICH THE
PUNGENT, BLUE SMOKE WAFTED ITS
WAY TOWARDS A HOLE IN THE ROOF. SINCE NONE OF THE
INTERNAL WALLS REACHED UP TO THE CEILING,
PEOPLE'S CLOTHES, BEDDING AND HAIR WOULD HAVE
BEEN AS SMOKY AS AN OLD KIPPER. AS SUCH, THE IDEA
OF AN UNPEATED WHISKY WOULD HAVE BEEN
UNTHINKABLE. IT JUST WOULDN'T HAVE BEEN WHISKY.

THE WHISKY HERITAGE OF ISLAY

IN ISLAY THERE HAS NEVER BEEN A SHORTAGE OF WATER FOR DISTILLING. ALTHOUGH THE ISLAND IS PRETTY LOW LYING WITH EVEN ITS HIGHEST HILLS LESS THAN 1,500 FEET, IT IS STILL HIGH ENOUGH TO SCRAPE THE BOTTOM OF ANY PASSING RAIN CLOUD. THESE REGULARLY ROLL IN OFF THE ATLANTIC TO KEEP THE BURNS, RIVERS AND BOGS WELL TOPPED UP. IF THE SOUND OF TRICKLING WATER IS WHAT DREW THE FIRST DISTILLERS TO A PARTICULAR SPOT, THOSE ON ISLAY WOULD HAVE BEEN SPOILT FOR CHOICE.

Of course Islay shares this damp, maritime climate with the rest of the Western Isles, but what does, or did, make it unique is access to that other vital ingredient – barley. Arable farming on Islay may not make much economic sense nowadays, but it is the most fertile of all the Hebrides. It originally grew enough cereal to get the island's whisky makers off to a good start before the first imported grain arrived in 1815. How much of the local crop was actually barley is hard to tell – not that the early distillers would have been too bothered. It was probably just as often oats or wheat, and doubtless sweetened with wild mint, thyme, bog myrtle and anything to make the potent brew more palatable.

The amount of whisky distilled on the island's farms depended on the harvest. In good years there was plenty of grain for both whisky and food, but in poor years it could result in famine. The authorities had always tried to control whisky making and, since the Act of Union of 1707, taxing it had been viewed as a key source of revenue in Scotland, but it proved hugely unpopular. When the prominent Glasgow MP Daniel Campbell voted in favour of the Malt Tax in 1725, the mob burned his house down. With the compensation paid out by the city fathers, Campbell bought Islay for £6,000 and, together with his descendants, helped modernize farming on the island.

OPPOSITE The Lagavulin distillery, as seen from across Lagavulin Bay, on the southern shores of Islay.

BELOW Everard's Sliding Rule, 1739 – an invaluable tool for gaugers, or excisemen, to determine the volume of spirit in a cask and therefore how much tax was due.

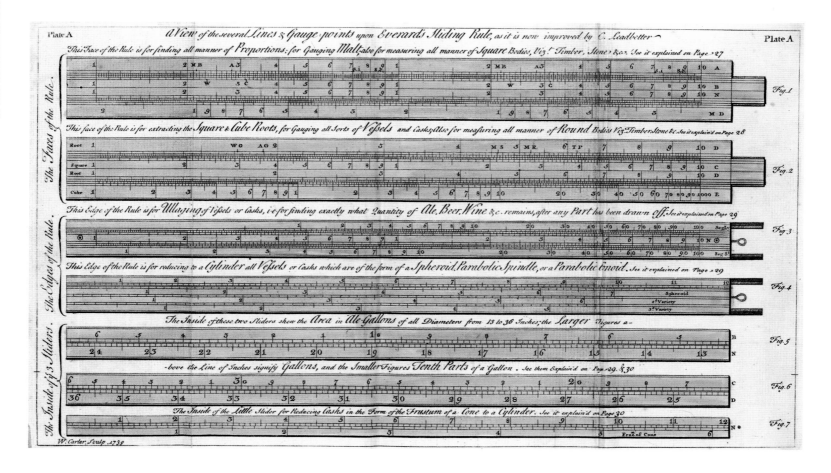

THE GAUGER IS COMING

For all the desire to raise tax, it took 90 years after the Union for the first exciseman, or "gauger", to reach Islay. By that point there was a vibrant cottage industry of illicit distillation and whisky smuggling to the mainland, though quite when it all began is anyone's guess. With the coast of Ireland less than 30 miles to the south, some have wondered if the secret of distillation may have been brought to Islay along with Catholicism by those sixth-century Irish monks in their coracles. But until some evidence is unearthed from a peat bog, we will never know. What is true is that whisky making was certainly well established before the island got its first licensed distillery at Bowmore in 1779. Other survivors out of over 20 distilleries founded during the nineteenth century are Laphroaig, Lagavulin and Ardbeg.

ROYAL COMMAND

Word of the island's unique whisky reached the Royal Household who, in the 1840s, twice requested "a cask of your best Islay Mountain Dew" from the Campbells. The demand for such whiskies continued into the early twentieth century, thanks to men like Sir Peter Mackie. The whisky baron and father of "White Horse" was a lifelong fan of Islay, owned Lagavulin, and tried to acquire Laphroaig. Yet by then the vast majority of the island's malts was disappearing into blends.

The blenders clearly rated the flavours of Islay malts and were willing to pay a premium for the extra costs involved, but they viewed the whiskies as a "top dressing" to be used sparingly. If the malt was particularly robust and smoky, more than a spoonful in a bottle of a typical Scotch blend would be too much. By contrast such a whisky might contain a third or more of Speyside malt.

As throughout Scotland, the fate of individual malt distilleries was completely tied to the fortunes of blended Scotch. When the whisky industry was full of confidence and forecasting strong growth for the future, production would be cranked up. Whenever these predictions proved over-optimistic and there was a surfeit of Scotch on the market, production slowed to a few days a week or even stopped altogether. This issue was compounded on Islay by the steady contraction in the number of big

BELOW The Islay Festival of Music and Malt is held in the last week of May every year, and celebrated its thirtieth anniversary in 2016.

distillers. If a whisky giant gobbled up a rival and found it now owned two distilleries there, it would often close one of them.

However, being on an island and relatively remote helped mothballed distilleries survive. During the long years waiting for an upturn, there was less risk of demolition and being buried beneath a car park or supermarket, as has sometimes happened on the mainland. But what really turned Islay's fortunes around was the rediscovery of single malts that began a generation ago.

Each of the island's seven historic distilleries, plus the boutique newcomer – Kilchoman, founded in 2005, has built a strong identity through their single malts. Names like Lagavulin, Bruichladdich and Ardbeg, that were once virtually unknown outside the Scotch whisky industry, are now world famous. Meanwhile, encouraged by events like the annual Islay Festival of Music and Malt, the number of whisky pilgrims to the island grows every year. If you like your whisky strong and pungent with the tarry, bittersweet flavours of peat smoke, this is the place to come.

BELOW Portnahaven, the westernmost village on Islay – next stop Newfoundland, over 3,000 miles away. The lighthouse is on the neighbouring tiny island of Orsay.

ABOVE Islay's most northerly distillery is the island's odd one out, since Bunnahabhain has traditionally been unpeated.

ARDBEG

ARDBEG, ISLE OF ISLAY, ARGYLL AND BUTE

ARDBEG IS THE FURTHEST FLUNG OF THE THREE DISTILLERIES IN THE KIDALTON AREA ON ISLAY'S SOUTH-EAST COAST, THE OTHERS BEING LAPHROAIG AND LAGAVULIN. WITH THE KINTYRE PENINSULA ON THE MAINLAND JUST 15 MILES BY BOAT, THE AREA HAD LONG BEEN A HOT-BED OF WHISKY SMUGGLING, AS A KILDALTON PARISH REPORT FROM THE 1770S MAKES CLEAR: "WE HAVE NOT AN EXCISE OFFICER IN THE WHOLE ISLAND. THE QUANTITY THEREFORE OF WHISKY MADE HERE IS VERY GREAT; AND THE EVIL THAT FOLLOWS DRINKING TO EXCESS OF THIS LIQUOR, IS VERY VISIBLE ON THIS ISLAND."

In 1798 the McDougalls – a family of tenant farmers, took out a lease to farm here, and John McDougall was probably distilling whisky before Ardbeg was officially founded in 1815. His son Alexander became a well-known figure in the Glasgow spirits trade and built Ardbeg's reputation there. He was fiercely proud of his name and once paid the fine of a fellow clansman in court on the grounds it was impossible for a McDougall to do wrong.

By the time of his death in 1853, Ardbeg was supporting a 200-strong community which soon had its own school. Ownership of the distillery passed to Alexander's sisters, Margaret and Flora, who were entered in a lease at the time as "co-partners" carrying on business at Ardbeg as distillers under the firm of Alexander MacDougall & Co. Whether they really were "Scotland's first lady distillers" is hard to know, for the old laird's former coachman was also down as managing the distillery. This was Colin Hay, who became owner of Ardbeg on the demise of the sisters, and continued to send the whisky to Buchanan's – a firm of whisky merchants in Glasgow who later became partners in the distillery.

FROM LONELY TO ALLIED

When the Victorian whisky writer Alfred Barnard visited in the 1880s he spoke of the distillery's lonely position on the very verge of the sea and how "the isolation tends to heighten the romantic sense of its position". From its pair of spirit stills it was then producing 250,000 gallons of Pure Islay Malt a year, which Buchanan's sold on to the big wine and spirit merchants in Glasgow, Liverpool and London. In the space of 50 years it had grown from a small farmyard operation pumping out just 500 gallons a week into a relatively big, full-fledged distillery with a staff of 60.

The firm of Alexander MacDougall & Co. carried on until the 1950s, the distillery having been bought

outright from the laird of Kildalton in the 1920s for £19,000. In 1973 Ardbeg was swallowed up by the Canadian giant Hiram Walker and the Distillers Company, with the former gaining full control four years later. In turn Hiram Walker became part of Allied Distillers, who also owned its near neighbour, Laphroaig.

Allied's MD, the late Alistair Cunningham, reportedly described Ardbeg as "heaven's own nectar", and said that "if you knew exactly the amount to take each day you could live for ever". Despite that, Ardbeg was essentially a blending ingredient, and its main role was to give the smooth, bestselling Ballantine's brand a slight smoky edge. Only Laphroaig was pushed as a single malt, and when the Scotch industry entered a prolonged slump in the 1980s, its owners decided they could live without two

BELOW Given the almost cult-like status of Ardbeg among fans of peat-soaked Islay malts, it is hard to believe that the distillery almost vanished in the 1980s at the height of the whisky loch was at its peak.

Islay distilleries. Ardbeg ceased production in 1982, then reopened in 1989 only to close again in 1996, possibly for ever. Empty and forlorn with its pagoda roof encased in scaffolding, it looked as if Ardbeg had reached the end of the road.

In 1997 it was bought for £7.1 million by the Glenmorangie company, who had to spend a few more million on repairs. The new owners acquired the aged stock, but there were serious holes in the inventory. In 2004 they were able to release a six-year-old "Very Young" Ardbeg, followed by "Still Young" and "Almost There", until finally they were able to launch a regular, 10-year-old flagship malt. Given the trend towards removing age-statements altogether from single malts, you wonder if Ardbeg's owners would have been so concerned today.

MORE SMOKE WITH NO FAN

The gaps in Ardbeg's warehouse have led to some creative blending between vintages and a profusion of different, limited-release expressions with varying degrees of peaty-ness. Along the way there has been Ardbeg Blasda – a third as smoky as the standard 10-year-old, and the intensely phenolic Ardbeg Supernova. Meanwhile cask strength expressions have included Uigedal, named after one of the lochs that supply Ardbeg's water, and "Alligator", matured in heavily re-charred Bourbon barrels. It has all helped to build the brand's cult status among its devotees, as has the Ardbeg Committee. This fan club

was founded in 2000 and meets by the ancient Kildalton Cross at midnight, or so it is said.

Ardbeg has a reputation for being one of the smokiest whiskies of all with its flavours of soot and tar, though there are a number of lighter expressions that challenge that. Its original distillers certainly knew of the importance of local peat, which was used to fuel the kiln and malt the barley until the 1960s. This was typical practice, but what set Ardbeg apart was the absence of fans in the pagoda roof to draw the smoke through the barley. As a result the grain was drenched in peat smoke for that much longer. Today the malt comes from the nearby Port Ellen maltings and, interestingly, the level of peat smoke is more or less the same as for Laphroaig and Lagavulin.

What sets all three apart is the way they are distilled, the shape of the stills and the differences in maturation. One reason why Ardbeg can cope with such highly peated malt is the curious piece of copper tubing attached to the wash still which helps purify the wash before sending it through to the spirit still. It is claimed that if you put Ardbeg's wash through a standard spirit still, the result would be undrinkable. The increased contact with the copper gives a faint sweetness to the spirit to balance the smoke.

BELOW "The isolation tends to heighten the romantic sense of its position," wrote Alfred Barnard on his visit to Ardbeg in the 1880s.

WHISKY TASTING NOTES
ARDBEG UIGEADAIL 54.2% ABV

Pronounced "Oog-a-dal" and named after the loch that supplies Ardbeg's water, Uigeadail is a vatting of the traditional 10-year-old with older malts that have been matured in sherry casks. The combination of the resinous, citrus peel notes from the sherry with the typical peat-soaked flavours of Ardbeg 10 is nothing if not intense, especially if sipped neat at cask strength. Yet even without water this earthy, mouth-filling dram is surprisingly smooth. It has a leathery texture and notes of spice, black treacle, liquorice and tar, but manages to maintain a fine balance of smoke and sweetness on the tongue. With a little water the smoke seems to intensify. In a word, it's a big whisky, and not for the faint-hearted.

BOWMORE

BOWMORE, ISLE OF ISLAY, ARGYLL AND BUTE

FOR THE RESIDENTS OF BOWMORE, THE ISLAND'S CAPITAL, THE LOCAL DISTILLERY IS THE FIRST LINE OF DEFENCE AGAINST THE ATLANTIC STORMS THAT OCCASIONALLY BLOW IN THROUGH THE OPEN JAWS OF LOCH INDAAL. ITS WAREHOUSES ARE LITERALLY BUILT INTO THE HARBOUR WALL, AND ARE OFTEN BATHED IN SEA SPRAY IF NOT BATTERED BY THE WAVES THEMSELVES. "THE DISTILLERY'S PROXIMITY TO THE SEA PLAYS A VITAL ROLE IN SHAPING THE FINAL CHARACTER OF OUR SPIRIT, WHICH BREATHES IN THE SALTY SEA AIR ALL THE WHILE IT'S MATURING," DECLARES THE BOWMORE WEBSITE.

Sniff deeply and take a sip, and there is something brisk and saline in this maritime malt, though no chemical analysis has ever revealed any trace of salt in the whisky. Most of Islay's distillers age their malts on the mainland and would tell you that where they are matured is of little consequence to the finished product. To which Bowmore might respond: "Well, they would say that, wouldn't they?" Bowmore sits on some 27,000 casks in its three warehouses.

What is beyond question is that Bowmore is the oldest surviving distillery on Islay; indeed it is one of the oldest in Scotland. It was founded in 1779, barely a decade after this pretty whitewashed village was established by Daniel Campbell, the laird of Islay whose grandfather

bought the island in 1726. The distillery quickly became a focal point for the community, along with the church, which is famously round. It was built that way, allegedly, to deny the devil any corner where he might hide and lure any unwitting member of the congregation into sin.

The Bowmore distillery was founded at the bottom of Hill Street down by the water-front by a local entrepreneur, John Simpson. He came from a nearby village at the foot of Loch Indaal, and had been granted rights to open a quarry and build houses here as well as cut turf from the moss. He was also the local postmaster, ran a steam packet from Port Askaig to Tarbert on the mainland, and there is even some evidence that he did some distilling on Jura as well.

OPPOSITE A traditional dunnage warehouse beside Bowmore – one of three used to age around 27,000 casks of its whisky. How maturation on the island effects the final flavour is hard to quantify.

BELOW Distilled right on the edge of Loch Indaal, Bowmore is a true maritime malt whose casks soak in the salty sea spray from the air, or so it is claimed.

BROTHERS MAKE BOWMORE GROW

How important the distillery was among Simpson's various business ventures is unclear, and Bowmore probably remained very small scale until it was acquired by twin brothers William and James Mutter in 1837. These Glasgow merchants of German extraction were determined to drag the distillery into the industrial age and expand the market for its whisky. James Mutter happened to be the Glaswegian vice-consul for the Ottoman Empire, Portugal and Brazil.

The still-house was expanded and new kilns and warehouses were added, while the number of stills had grown to four by the 1880s. According to a contemporary etching these were all different and included a weird double-headed still that fed into two separate worm tubs – a radical design that never caught on. Because of the expansion, the water supply that came from the River Laggan had to be diverted into a nine-mile aqueduct to carry sufficient water to feed the mash. At the time production of this "pure Islay malt" had risen to 200,000 gallons a year, making Bowmore second only to Ardbeg in scale. The Mutters had their own 145-ton steamship to carry the casks to the mainland, where it was aged and bottled under the arches of Glasgow's Central Station. Some of it was exported as far afield as Canada.

But something went wrong, and by 1890 the Mutter family had gone out of business. Over the next 70 years a number of new owners came and went, but the distillery kept going, except during the Second World War when it was requisitioned by Coastal Command. After this brief interlude as a base for flying boats on U-boat patrol in the Atlantic, Bowmore was back making whisky. In 1963 it was bought by the Glasgow-based whisky brokers Stanley P. Morrison Ltd, who began to crank up production. Within five years the distillery was pumping out 880,000 gallons per annum – 14 times what it had produced the year before the sale. The firm, which became known as Morrison Bowmore, soon realized what an asset it had. Its business had been all about selling bulk whisky to blenders; now it began to focus on single malts.

FLOOR MALTINGS

Bowmore took the bold decision to hang on to its own floor maltings at a time when most distilleries were abandoning theirs as an expensive anachronism. Today they only provide a third of the malt needed, but they give Bowmore a real traditional feel. Having been steeped in water, the barley is spread evenly over the stone malting floors, of which there are three. As the grain starts to warm up and begin germinating, it has to be turned every four hours to prevent it matting together. Then, after about a week, it is transported to a wire mesh above the malt kiln to be dried. The dense blue peat smoke weaves its way through the malt and out through the slats in the pagoda roof.

Floor maltings give the distillery a self-sufficient feel, though whether they have any material impact on the final whisky would be difficult to prove. Their main role is really about enhancing the visitor experience, which they undoubtedly do. Somehow the next distillery, with its pagoda roof just there for decoration and completely free of smoke, will never be quite as evocative. And with this in mind, Bowmore were one of the first distilleries to install a visitor's centre.

Those on a distillery tour will hear about warehouse number one, partly below sea level and the oldest in Scotland. They will also hear of the curious fate of warehouse number three which is now the local swimming pool and heated by the waste heat from the still-room next door. Then comes a chance to taste and possibly buy some of the malts. The range was revamped in 2007 and includes "Legend", "Darkest" and a whole raft of aged expressions up to 40-year-old and beyond.

WHISKY TASTING NOTES
BOWMORE 12-YEAR-OLD 40% ABV

Like Macallan, this famous distillery – the oldest on Islay – has gone the route of non-age-statement whiskies like Bowmore "Legend" and "Small Batch", but the 12-year-old remains the real flagship whisky and a popular choice for those who want to explore a more subtle side of the island. True to its Islay roots, there is an immediate waft of peat from the glass, but there is a softer, herbal element to the smoke. It is less astringent and medicinal than Islay malts like Laphroaig or Ardbeg. When tasted with a little water, it won't put hairs on your chest like some Islay peat monsters, but you can enjoy this moderately smoky whisky with a beguiling citrus freshness and a light, silky texture.

BRUICHLADDICH

BRUICHLADDICH, ISLE OF ISLAY, ARGYLL AND BUTE

FOR YEARS BRUICHLADDICH HAS REVELLED IN A SPIRIT OF DEFIANCE THAT OFFERS A COUNTERBLAST TO ALL THAT IS CORPORATE AND BLAND IN THE WORLD OF SCOTCH WHISKY. SINCE 2000, WHEN THE DISTILLERY WAS BOUGHT BY AN INDEPENDENT CONSORTIUM, IT HAS BEEN THE INDUSTRY'S ANSWER TO THOSE SELF-STYLED BAD BOYS OF BRITISH BREWING, SCOTLAND'S BREWDOG. BRUICHLADDICH'S INDEPENDENCE LASTED UNTIL 2012 WHEN IT WAS BOUGHT BY THE FRENCH SPIRITS GROUP REMY COINTREAU FOR £58 MILLION, THOUGH IT SEEMS THE OLD ETHOS REMAINS INTACT. ON ITS WEBSITE BRUICHLADDICH STILL DESCRIBES ITSELF AS A "PROGRESSIVE HEBRIDEAN DISTILLER" AND PROCLAIMS: "WE ARE PROUDLY NON-CONFORMIST AS HAS ALWAYS BEEN THE WAY."

Founded in 1881, Bruichladdich was a purpose-built distillery from the start. Instead of evolving out of the farm like so many others, it was a state-of-the-art whisky-making machine with modern cavity walls and concrete – a radical new building material at the time. The concrete was reinforced with pebbles from the sea shore. Built on a hill around a spacious courtyard, it was designed by Robert Harvey, a young engineer from Glasgow. He and his two elder brothers were part of the Glasgow-based whisky dynasty that owned Yoker and Dundas Hill – the largest malt distillery in Scotland at the time.

In the 1880s blended Scotch was really starting to take off, and the blenders were eager to source less dominant malts for the bulk of their blends. Rather than copy the traditional, heavily peated style of the likes of Lagavulin and Ardbeg, Bruichladdich strove to offer the blenders a less smoky, more approachable malt. The style of whisky was probably similar to Bunnahabhain, which was founded on Islay the same year. Soon Bruichladdich's two stills were pumping out 94,000 gallons of malt whisky a year. Every week the grain was shipped in and the barrels were shipped out in small, flat-bottomed steam puffers. Most was bought by the Distillers Company on the understanding that Bruichladdich did not try and bottle any single malt itself.

BRUICHLADDICH RUNS OUT OF STEAM

The distillery limped along, barely making a profit, until it closed in 1907 and remained so throughout the First World War. In 1919 Robert's nephew, Rudd Harvey, was out in Chile when he received a telegram from his father: "Come home 1st steamer, distillery working." In truth it was still idle and there were two-foot weeds growing in the courtyard

as Rudd discovered on his return. But the older generation of Harveys, who had by then lost their distilleries on the mainland, were keen to fire up the stills once more.

This they did until 1929, when Bruichladdich became a casualty of the Depression. A buyer was eventually found in Joseph Hobbs, a Scottish-born entrepreneur who had made and lost a fortune in the States. Hobbs paid just £8,000 in 1936 and then swiftly resold the distillery to another firm he had interests in for three times the amount. Then, having built up reasonable stocks, the distillery was sold again to the Glasgow whisky brokers Ross & Coulter for £205,000 in 1952.

BELOW Bruichladdich's master distiller, Jim McEwan with a cask sample from the distillery's warehouse. McEwan, who was born on the island and previously worked for Bowmore, has been a lifelong ambassador for Islay malts.

OPPOSITE The picturesque village of Port Charlotte on the shores of Loch Indaal, whose name has been adopted by nearby Bruichladdich for a separate range of malts.

By the late 1950s, with its old steam engine and the barley still hoisted up to the barley loft by horse, Bruichladdich was now far from state-of-the-art. More mergers and acquisitions followed, and the distillery's production capacity was doubled to 800,000 gallons with a second pair of stills. But in 1993 its then owners, the Glasgow-based blenders Whyte & Mackay, declared it was "surplus to requirement," and closed it down again. Technically the distillery had been "mothballed", with its equipment looked after as it waited for the cyclical upturn in Scotch whisky's fortunes, but as the years went by hopes of Bruichladdich's resurrection began to fade.

NEW OWNERS, NEW EXPRESSIONS

The distillery was rescued by a private consortium, led by the wine merchant and independent whisky bottler Mark Reynier, in December 2000. For £6.5 million they acquired a patchy collection of maturing stock and a distillery in desperate need of repair. The winter months were spent patching up the building and distilling equipment until the stills were fired up and the first new spirit flowed at the end of May 2001. At the party to celebrate the event, one very old Ileach, or native of Islay, was heard to say: "This is better than the Coronation."

Having poached Jim McEwan, veteran distiller and Ileach, from Bowmore, the new owners decided to distil, alongside the lighter Bruichladdich, a heavily peated spirit which they called Port Charlotte after a defunct distillery nearby. In the meantime they began to unleash a dizzying array of new expressions and limited releases to exploit what stocks they had in the warehouse. News of every new bottling, however small, was trumpeted to every blogger and whisky writer on the planet to help this remote, one-off distillery to punch above its weight.

Bruichladdich's owners were keen to make the whisky as much part of the island as possible. Initially it was bottled off the island, using Islay water that was sent over to reduce the whisky to bottling strength. In 2003 a bottling line was installed at the distillery and a year later this was followed by "Ugly Betty", Scotland's last surviving Lomond still. It was brought over from the mainland and is now used to make "The Botanist" gin. Jim McEwan and his team even produced an organic single malt made from locally grown "bere" barley.

Other bottlings included a pink whisky, X4 – a high-strength malt distilled four times – and Octomore, which was claimed to be "the most heavily peated whisky in the world". Finally in 2011, Mark Reynier was able to celebrate a decade of continual production at Bruichladdich by launching his first 10-year-old – The Laddie Ten. A year later he stepped down, leaving many of the old team including McEwan with the new French owners.

WHISKY TASTING NOTES
BRUICHLADDICH PORT CHARLOTTE
SCOTTISH BARLEY 50% ABV

Port Charlotte is the pretty village on the shore of Loch Indaal, two miles south of Bruichladdich, that was home to the Lochindaal distillery for a hundred years until 1929. By all accounts its whisky was drenched in peat, and this expression is Bruichladdich's tribute to it. Pale gold in colour, it certainly has a powerful peat reek, but with less of that iodine and medicinal character you find in the likes of Laphroaig. There is also a distinct burnt caramel sweetness on the nose and some may even detect a slight fruitiness. On the tongue there is a dusty, smoky herbal core which really dominates until other elements emerge including candied fruit and liquorice.

LAPHROAIG

PORT ELLEN, ISLE OF ISLAY, ARGYLL AND BUTE

AS A SINGLE MALT LAPHROAIG IS FAMED FOR ITS FEROCIOUSLY PUNGENT FLAVOUR — A MIX OF TAR, SEA SALT, IODINE AND SMOKE, BUT IF YOU VISIT THE ACTUAL DISTILLERY YOU MAY BE SLIGHTLY DISAPPOINTED. LYING IN ITS SHELTERED BAY WITH THE LOW HILLS OF KILDALTON BEHIND AND A GENTLY SHELVING SEA SHORE IN FRONT, IT IS CERTAINLY PRETTY. BUT IT DOESN'T QUITE LIVE UP TO THE WHISKY'S UNCOMPROMISING REPUTATION — A SINGLE MALT THAT YOU WILL EITHER "LOVE OR HATE", AS AN OLD ADVERTISING CAMPAIGN ONCE CLAIMED. OF COURSE IF YOUR TRIP TO LAPHROAIG WERE TO COINCIDE WITH A FULL-SCALE ATLANTIC STORM THAT WOULD BE DIFFERENT. WITH BREAKERS BATTERING THE WHITEWASHED WALLS OF THE DISTILLERY, IT WOULD FEEL LIKE THE PERFECT PLACE TO DRINK LAPHROAIG, RAW AND UNDILUTED.

The name comes from the Gaelic *Lag Bhròdhas*, which roughly translates as "hollow of the broad bay". It was here in the early nineteenth century that Donald and Alexander Johnston leased a thousand acres from the laird of Islay to farm cattle. Soon after, by around 1815, they were making whisky as well. It was a well-chosen spot with a good, consistent supply of water and peat, and Port Ellen just a few miles west. This was the main port on Islay's south coast, where barley could be brought in from the mainland and casks of whisky shipped out. Laphroaig was soon joined by the Ardenistiel distillery next door, which for a while belonged to James and Andrew Stein from the famous dynasty of Lowland distillers. By the 1860s it had been amalgamated into Laphroaig.

Long before then, Alexander Johnston sold his share of the business to his brother for £350 and emigrated to Australia. Donald struggled on alone until his death in 1847. According to some he drowned in a vat of his own bunt ale. The distillery was left in trust to his son Dugald, who was only 11 at the time. Ten years later he took over the running of Laphroaig with his first cousin. As the century progressed the pair started to complain about the raw deal they were getting from their agents – JL Mackie & Co., a firm of whisky merchants in Glasgow who also distributed and later owned Laphroaig's great rival, Lagavulin.

FOUL PLAY

This rivalry began to turn sour in 1887, when the Johnstons, who were making a loss at the time, decided to terminate the relationship with Mackie's. By that stage Peter Mackie, who was to become one of the great late Victorian whisky barons with the White Horse blend, was working for his uncle's firm. He was deeply attached to Islay whisky and somewhat obsessed with

Laphroaig. He fell out with the Johnstons over water rights and ended up in court, having ordered one of his men to choke off Laphroaig's water supply using stones in 1907. The following year Mackie decided to build a replica of the distillery within the ground of Lagavulin which he christened the Malt Mill. Yet despite replicating the stills as carefully as he could, and employing Laphroaig's former head brewer, he never managed to copy the whisky.

When Laphroaig's lease came up for renewal in 1921, Mackie made one final, failed bid to buy the distillery. Instead it remained in the family with a direct descendant, Ian Hunter, who set about expanding capacity with two new spirit stills, a new

BELOW LEFT As one of a handful distilleries to retain its floor maltings, Laphroaig's kiln infuses the grain with dense, blue, peat smoke, although most of its malt comes ready peated from Port Ellen.

BELOW Sir Peter Mackie – or "Restless Peter" as he was known, was the whisky baron with the greatest attachment to malt whisky, particularly from Islay. He owned neighbouring Lagavulin and built a copy of Laphroaig in its grounds, though he never managed to replicate the whisky.

OPPOSITE Laphroaig – "the finest whisky in the world", or so Prince Charles is said to have claimed.

VANITY FAIR Supplement.

"Restless Peter."

wash still and a new maltings. With the US officially teetotal since the advent of Prohibition in 1919, Hunter was one of the first in the Scotch whisky industry to bring in old Bourbon barrels for ageing his spirit. At the time most other distillers in Scotland were using old sherry butts from Spain. The coconut and vanilla flavours of American oak have helped soften the bitter, peat-soaked character of Laphroaig's new-make spirit ever since.

THE LADY LOVES LAPHROAIG

In the early 1930s Bessie Williamson, who had just graduated from Glasgow University, took a summer job at Laphroaig to help out with admin. She arrived with a single suitcase, but ended up staying for 40 years. With her boss suffering a stroke in 1938 and confined to a wheelchair, she took over as distillery manager – a unique position in an industry dominated by men.

Production was paused during the Second World War, but afterwards the stills were fired up and in 1954 Williamson inherited Laphroaig on the death of Ian Hunter, who had no next of kin. She continued to sell the whisky to blenders and as a single malt, particularly the US, where a certain amount of Laphroaig had been sold legally as a medicinal spirit during Prohibition. In an early BBC interview she explained that "the secret of Islay whiskies is the peaty water and the peat". She also spoke of an

increasing demand among whisky drinkers for the island's malts which Laphroaig was struggling to supply.

During the 1960s Williamson gradually sold the business to Long John Distillers which was part of the American group Shenley Industries, but continued as distillery manager until her retirement in 1972. Three years later Long John was bought by the brewer Whitbread, who later sold their whisky business to Allied Domecq. Laphroaig then passed back into American ownership in 2005, when it was bought by the owners of Jim Beam, and now belongs to the Japanese as part of Beam-Suntory. Today its Scotch whisky stable-mates include the Teacher's blend and fellow Islay malt Bowmore.

Despite all the changes in ownership, Laphroaig appears in rude health with its Royal coat of arms received from Prince Charles proudly displayed on the label for over two decades. The Prince came in person to do the honours in 1994 and by the time he got to the distillery he may well have needed a drink, having crash-landed the Royal plane on the island's tiny runway. "I hope you continue to use the traditional methods," he apparently told Ian Henderson, the then distillery manager. "I think you make the finest whisky in the world." Among the traditional methods is the continued use of floor maltings which account for a quarter of Laphroaig's needs.

WHISKY TASTING NOTES
LAPHROAIG QUARTER CASK 48% ABV

Some years ago Laphraoig decided to revive an old tradition in its warehouses on Islay. Having aged in traditional ex-bourbon barrels used for the distillery's flagship 10-year-old single malt, some is filled into casks a quarter of the normal size which increases the ratio of wood to whisky by a third and therefore speeds up the whole maturation process. However, the effect does not seem to diminish Laphroaig's burst of tarry peat and iodine that the distillery is well known for. Maybe there is an extra layer of vanilla sweetness on the nose, and this becomes more apparent on the tongue, giving a slightly richer texture to the whisky before some dry wood tannins poke through on its lingering finish.

LAGAVULIN
LAGAVULIN, ISLE OF ISLAY, ARGYLL AND BUTE

LAGAVULIN SITS IN THE MIDDLE OF THE SO-CALLED "KILDALTON THREE" WITH ARDBEG A MILE TO THE EAST, AND LAPHROAIG ROUND THE NEXT BAY TO THE WEST. FOR A WHILE SUCH CLOSE PROXIMITY BRED CONTEMPT, OR AT LEAST FIERCE RIVALRY BETWEEN LAGAVULIN AND LAPHROAIG, BUT THAT HAS LONG MELLOWED INTO MUTUAL RESPECT. EACH PRODUCES FINE SINGLE MALTS WITH A HEFTY BITTERSWEET TANG OF PEAT, YET DESPITE BEING NEXT-DOOR NEIGHBOURS THEIR WHISKIES ARE DECIDEDLY DIFFERENT.

Across Lagavulin Bay are the ruins of Dunyvaig Castle, which was once a stronghold of the Lord of the Isles. They kept a fleet of flat-bottomed boats, good for slipping in and out past a vicious set of rocks that lurk just beneath the surface at high tide and guard the entrance to the bay. Adding to the sense of history is the fact that Robert the Bruce is said to have fled here after his defeat by the Earl of Pembroke in the fourteenth century. As for whisky making, that too goes back a long way.

The whisky writer Dave Broom has speculated that this corner of Islay may have been the crucible of distilling in Scotland. When Áine Ó Catháin married Angus MacDonald, Lord of the Isles, in 1300 her wedding party concluded at Dunyvaig Castle. She brought with her the MacBeatha family who became

the hereditary physicians to the MacDonalds and who did know the secret of *UisgeBeatha*, the water of life.

Whether some evidence will ever come to light remains to be seen, but what is clear is that by the mid-eighteenth century this strip of coastline was a seething hot-bed of illicit distillation. It appears there was a kind of whisky-making co-operative, with "ten small and separate smuggling bothys for the manufacture of moonlight", to quote Alfred Barnard on his distilleries tour of 1887. Each had its own primitive still, and they were all clustered round a mill that supplied the malted barley.

MILLS IN A HOLLOW

Out of this emerged Lagavulin whose name comes from the Gaelic *lagganmhouillin* or mill in the hollow.

LEFT Officially founded in 1816, Laphroaig's roots may be considerable older. Some claim it was once part of a collection of small smuggling botheys dedicated to 'the manufacture of moonshine'

BELOW The spirits safe – a common feature in all malt whisky distilleries through which freshly-condensed spirit flows, and where the distiller makes the 'final cut' that will be filled into cask.

The distillery was founded in 1816 by John Johnston, father of Donald Johnston of Laphroaig. A year later another small distillery founded by the laird, Archibald Campbell, cropped up alongside, and appears to have traded under the name Ardmore during its brief life. It was merged into Lagavulin when Johnston died in 1836 owing money to Alexander Graham, a Glasgow merchant who was married to a local girl.

Graham ran the Islay Cellar with his partner James Logan Mackie, and acquired Lagavulin and a lease on the land for the princely sum of £1,103 9s.8d. The pair were also sole agents for Laphroaig and sold both whiskies as pure Islay malt in and around the Glasgow area. When James Mackie's nephew Peter joined the business in 1878 he was packed off to Lagavulin to study the art of distillation. By all accounts he fell in love with the island and its heavily peated malts.

On his return, Peter Mackie wasted no time in promoting Lagavulin and Laphroaig to a wider audience, while developing trade sales to blenders. By 1884 demand was such that he was able to open an office in London. Back on Islay, Lagavulin was expanded into one of the biggest distilleries on the island with three malt houses and two kilns and an annual production of 75,000 gallons. According to Alfred Barnard, the whisky was floated out in barrels across the bay to ships waiting beyond the rocks.

BACKING A WINNER

In 1890 Mackie trademarked the name of the blend that was to make his fortune. At first White Horse was sold only abroad, but once exports had reached 24,000 cases a year, it was decided to launch the brand in the UK in 1901. By the outbreak of the First World War annual domestic sales were running at 70,000 cases. There was grain whisky and Speyside malt in the blend, but there was always a decent dollop of Lagavulin, which became the spiritual home of White Horse.

Known as "Restless Peter" to his staff, Sir Peter Mackie was the quintessential Scotsman on the make. Having squabbled with his neighbours he tried to make a "Laphroaig-style" whisky from 1908 at the Malt Mill distillery which sat within the grounds of Laphroaig. It was about a fifth the size in terms of production, and reputedly used heather in the mash, along with heavily peated malt. According to Dr Nick Morgan of Lagavulin's parent company Diageo: "As far as anyone knows it was nothing like Laphroaig, albeit it was a pretty good whisky for blending, so they carried on

making it for over 50 years."

One rare blend from the 1930s and 1940s that did contain Malt Mill was Mackie's Ancient Scotch, which gives the distillery as its address. If you have a bottle of it lurking in the back of your drinks cupboard, it could be worth a few thousand pounds. But if you produced some Malt Mill itself, nobody would believe you. It appears it was never bottled as a single malt. At Lagavulin there is one bottle of Malt Mill's new make spirit, sealed with a lump of wax and with a label scribbled in biro. It is believed to be unique, but it's not Scotch whisky, having spent no time in wood.

The Malt Mill closed in 1962 and its two stills were absorbed into Lagavulin. Around that time, the old floor maltings were closed in favour of the Port Ellen maltings nearby. Port Ellen produced its own single malt until it was closed as a distillery in 1983. Five years later, Lagavulin 16-year-old was selected as one of the original six "Classic Malts", whose success guaranteed the distillery's survival. Lagavulin did not completely escape the slow-down in Scotch whisky in the 1980s, and the distillery was put on a three-day week, causing serious supply issues down the line. Thanks to the popularity of its malts, which now include a 12-year-old and a Distiller's Edition, production has long been running at full steam.

WHISKY TASTING NOTES
LAGAVULIN 16-YEAR-OLD 43% ABV

Diageo's accountants may rue the day it was decided to fill Lagavulin as a 16-year-old single malt and present it as one of the founder members of the six Classic Malts. But the angels up above must be happy to get their 2% share through evaporation every year, and so too are the whisky's many fans. The prolonged maturation helps tame the medicinal, peat-soaked aromas and give them an extra dimension. Beneath the smoke something more exotic and subtle starts to emerge – a mix of beach bonfires, Lapsang Souchong tea and candied peel. It is a magnificent brute that rolls over the tongue, at first oily and luscious but turning drier and almost mineral with a salty maritime finish.

BELOW For its flagship single malt, the casks of Lagavulin slumber for sixteen long years.

THE OTHER DISTILLERIES OF ISLAY

WHEN PORT ELLEN WAS CLOSED IN 1983, THE OMENS DID NOT LOOK GOOD FOR ISLAY'S SURVIVING DISTILLERIES. ARDBEG AND BRUICHLADDICH LOOKED PARTICULARLY VULNERABLE, BUT TODAY BOTH ARE IN RUDE HEALTH ALONG WITH THE ISLAND'S THREE OTHER DISTILLERIES YET TO BE MENTIONED.

LOOKING EAST

The oldest is *Caol Ila*, which lies partially hidden in a cove, just up the coast from Port Askaig opposite Jura. It was built in 1846 by a Glasgow distiller called Hector Henderson and was producing enough whisky by the 1880s for David MacBrayne's steamers to call twice a week at the distillery's own pier. Grain would be delivered and the full casks taken away to be blended up or sold on by its owners Bulloch Lade & Co. of Glasgow.

The firm was once a serious competitor to the Distillers Company (DCL), but in 1920 it went into voluntary liquidation and was gobbled up by DCL a few years later. In the 1970s, Caol Ila was completely rebuilt and expanded to carry on its sole purpose in life – that of supplying a moderately peated Islay malt to big-selling blends like Johnnie Walker. The refurbishment left Caol Ila by far the biggest distillery on Islay and responsible for a quarter of the island's malt. And while it did no favours to the distillery aesthetically, it did leave those working in the still-room with one of the best views in the industry. Through the giant plate-glass windows can be seen the shimmering waters of the Sound of Islay, the occasional playful seal and the Paps of Jura beyond.

Caol Ila has slowly emerged from the blended shadows with its own single malt. Other than an occasional release under the old Flora & Fauna range and the odd independent bottling, there was no regular expression until the 12-year-old in 2002. Three years on it became part of the expanded "Classic Malts". Over the years the distillery has played around with non-peated malts, starting with Caol Ila Highland in the 1980s, which was purely for blending.

BELOW Caol Ila, Islay's biggest distillery, is responsible for a quarter of the whisky produced on the island. It was almost entirely rebuilt in the 1970s

A SALTY SEA-DOG

Four miles up the coast from Caol Ila is Islay's most northerly distillery of *Bunnahabhain* – Gaelic for "the mouth of the river". It was founded by the Greenlees brothers in 1881, the same year as Bruichladdich, and entailed the building of a road, a row of cottages for the distillery workers, a schoolroom and a pier. Yet despite the £30,000 spent by the Islay Distillery Co., Bunnahabhain was making a profit of £10,000 by year two. The directors were delighted and told their new distillery manager, Mr Smith, to name his terms. His salary was set at £350 with free lodging and keep for a cow, and his request for "not
less than £30 to be spent on furniture" was duly granted.

Five years later the distillery became a founding part of Highland Distillers, which eventually became part of the Edrington Group in 1999. Bunnahabhain's new owners were determined to focus on their core brands of Macallan, Highland Park and The Famous Grouse, and in 2003 decided their one Islay distillery was surplus to requirements. It was bought by Burn Stewart Distillers, which was itself acquired by the South African drinks group Distell in 2013.

Over the years, Bunnahabhain has been quite low profile with its gentle style of whisky, which offers none of the phenolic bitterness of an Ardbeg or Laphroaig, though it does share a brisk maritime character with the rest of Islay's malts. The decision to use little if any peat was clearly to make the malt more attractive to blenders, though its current owners are keen to develop the distillery's single malts.

"Bunnahabhain is not a typical, heavily peated, smoke-filled Islay," declares the website. "Instead it lets the sea and the island's nature speak naturally." As well as a raft of aged expressions from 12-year-old to 40-year-old, it has started experimenting with peated versions like *Cruach-Mhòna*, which literally means peat stack.

Bunnahabhain's label features a salty sea-dog, one hand on the wheel of his boat, the other shielding his eyes from the sun. There is no bottle of Scotch poking from his pocket and he looks in control. This was clearly not the case with the skipper of the *Wyre Majestic* trawler that hit the rocks and nearly took out the pier in October 1974. He was blamed for being down below at an "inappropriate time", though the Mate claimed the skipper may have been at the wheel in a "stupor".

WHISKY TASTING NOTES
CAOL ILA 12-YEAR-OLD 43% ABV

This distillery, a relatively big one by Islay standards, is a fairly recent entrant among single malts. In the last decade its owners have promoted it quite strongly to ease the pressure of demand on the likes of Lagavulin. With its pale straw colour Caol Ila starts off a little subdued on the nose. The peat smoke is certainly there, but it is more fragrant than pungent, and there is also a youthful, malty aroma. Yet as you swirl it round in your glass and perhaps add a drop or two of water, it becomes more complex with notes of wax, soap and even olives. Tasted neat, there is an oily sweetness which dries on adding water to reveal traces of sea salt.

LEFT There has been a pier at Bunnahabhain for as long as there has been a distillery.

LEFT How much ageing whisky in situ affects its character is hard to prove, but those who do mature their spirit on the island swear that it does make a difference.

ABOVE Islay's youngest distillery, founded in 2005, is a link back to its farm distilling past. From using local barley to ageing the whisky on site, Kilchoman controls the process from start to finish.

THE WESTERN FARM

Over on the other side of the island is the island's youngest whisky-making venture – *Kilchoman*, a tiny boutique distillery founded in 2005 by Anthony Wills. From the start every drop of spirit was destined to be single malt, with everything possible sourced from the island. Wills refers to it as Islay's farm distillery, with barley from the fields around the distillery and the whisky bottled by hand on site. The grain is floor malted and dried over a peat kiln.

To be Scotch whisky the spirit has to mature for at least three years in wood, an agonizing wait for any new distiller waiting for his first sale. By all accounts Kilchoman's survival was touch and go at times, but in 2009 it was able to release 8,450 bottles of its Inaugural Release. Not so long ago to bottle a single malt, particularly something smoky from Islay, at less than ten years old would have been considered infanticide. However, from the level of peat smoke to making the mash and distilling the spirit and, above all, to carefully selecting the right wood, everything was done to create a spirit that was sufficiently mature at such a tender age. The following year 50,000 bottles were sold – a drop in the ocean compared to Glenlivet and Macallan, but proof that Kilchoman was here to stay. Given the popularity of Islay malts, there may well be other new distilleries.

Down the road from Bruichladdich is the village of *Port Charlotte*, whose distillery Lochindaal closed down in 1929 after a hundred years. At the time of writing 'Port Charlotte' only exists as a peaty expression of Bruichladdich, but planning permission has been granted for a distillery of that name, and there is talk of construction in 2016.

WHISKY TASTING NOTES
BUNNAHABHAIN 18-YEAR-OLD 46.3% ABV

Whisky lovers on Islay who need respite from all that high-octane peat have always had a refuge on the north of the island in the shape of Bunnahabhain, whose standard 12-year-old is a fine dram in itself. The 18-year-old is a real step upwards and brings a warming sherried character to Bunnahabhain's maritime house style. Take a sniff and think of sweet glacé cherries, caramel, dark chocolate ... and you won't be far wrong. On the tongue the rich sherry notes continue with plenty of active wood adding a vanilla edge to the burnt sugar and cherry fruit and a slightly chewy texture. There is distinct chocolate character as well that stays right through to the finish.

TOP The breast-like Paps of Jura at sunset, seen from the mainland.

LEFT The lost distillery of Port Charlotte, originally called Lochindaal, that made whisky, on and off for 100 years until it was bought and closed down by DCL in 1929. The name lives on through Bruichladdich who still use the distillery's old warehouses.

WESTERN ISLES

IT IS ONE OF THE GREAT, UNSOLVED MYSTERIES OF SCOTCH WHISKY THAT ISLAY IS AWASH WITH MALT DISTILLERIES YET THE REST OF THE WESTERN ISLES HAVE SO FEW. IN ITS ENTIRE HISTORY THIS NECKLACE OF ISLANDS, EXCLUDING ISLAY, WAS HOME TO JUST 13 LICENSED DISTILLERIES. SEVEN OF THEM WERE ON THE ISLE OF SKYE, WHICH NOW ONLY HAS TALISKER, WHILE THE ISLE OF MULL HAS JUST TOBERMORY, WHICH SPENT MUCH OF THE TWENTIETH CENTURY IN MOTHBALLS AND ONLY SURVIVED BY THE SKIN OF ITS TEETH. YET BOTH ARE NOW OPERATING AT FULL STEAM, AND SALES OF TALISKER ARE SAID TO BE BOOMING. IN RECENT YEARS THEY HAVE BEEN JOINED BY A NUMBER OF SMALL DISTILLERIES, STARTING WITH ARRAN IN 1995, FOLLOWED BY ABHAINN DEARG ON LEWIS AND, LATEST OF ALL, THE ISLE OF HARRIS DISTILLERY WHICH WENT INTO PRODUCTION IN 2015.

THE WHISKY HERITAGE OF THE WESTERN ISLES

WITH THE EXCEPTION OF ISLAY AND TIREE, THE POOR-QUALITY SOIL OF THE WESTERN ISLES HARDLY ENCOURAGED THE GROWING OF CROPS, WHICH COULD EASILY BE RUINED AFTER A RAIN-SODDEN HARVEST. THOUGH MAYBE IT WAS WATCHING THE WET GRAIN FERMENT OF ITS OWN ACCORD THAT FIRST SET THE ISLANDERS ON THE PATH TO WHISKY. SUCH NATURAL FERMENTATION WOULD HAVE PRODUCED A ROUGH, COARSE BEER THAT COULD ONLY BENEFIT FROM BEING BOILED UP AND PURIFIED INTO A SPIRIT. THERE WERE PLENTY WILLING TO HAVE A GO, AS JOHN KNOX (NO RELATION TO EDINBURGH'S SIXTEENTH-CENTURY FIRE AND BRIMSTONE PREACHER) WROTE OF MULL ON HIS HEBRIDEAN TOUR OF THE 1780S: "OF GRAIN, THIS COAST CANNOT RAISE, WITH THE GREATEST EXERTIONS, A SUFFICIENCY FOR THE USE OF THE INHABITANTS; AND OF EVERY YEAR'S PRODUCTION OF BARLEY, A THIRD OR FOURTH PART IS DISTILLED INTO A SPIRIT CALLED WHISKY, OF WHICH THE NATIVES ARE IMMODERATELY FOND."

Whisky drinking was entwined in the clan culture of the islands. Each clan would have its own bard who would wax lyrical about the generosity of the chief and his "overflowing cups of usquebaugh", or whisky. At times of celebration, a shell known as a Quaich would be passed round to share this precious nectar. The festivities would last for days with the elders of the clan sat round in a circle. It was claimed that they would drink until they passed out, at which point someone would carry them off in a barrow.

In 1609, James IV attempted to bring the Highland chiefs to heal and curb their competitive feasting with the Statutes of Iona, one of which dealt specifically with the "extraordinary drinking of strong wines and acquavitie". The elders and clan chief were allowed to import a limited quantity of wines and whiskies from the mainland, though the limits were generous. MacLean of Duart on Mull was allowed up to four tuns of wine a year, equivalent to about 18 bottles a day. Common people

LEFT An early map showing the necklace of islands that stretch round Scotland's coast to Orkney, beyond which lay the very edge of the known world, or what the Ancient Greeks christened *Ultima Thule*.

were denied all imported liquor, though they were allowed to brew their own beer and distil their own whisky for their own use.

A DIRE WARNING

By the time Martin Martin was touring the Hebrides to compile his *Description of the Western Islands of Scotland* of 1703, he found that the great, whisky-fuelled feasts of the clan chiefs were no longer happening. Yet the amount of whisky that people drank and the strength of it certainly caught his eye as can be seen from the following passage about the Isle of Lewis:

The corn grown here is barley, oats and rye … Natives brew several sorts of liquors; as common Uisquebaugh, another called Trestarig, id est Aqua Vitae, three times distilled, which is strong and hot; a third sort is four times distilled Usquebaugh-baul which at first taste affects all the Members of the Body: two spoonfuls of this last Liquor is a sufficient Dose; and if any Man exceed this, it would presently stop his Breath, and endanger his Life. The Trestarig and Usquebaugh-baul, are both made of Oats.

The life-threatening properties of usquebaugh-baul may be a slight exaggeration, but Martin was probably right about the process. Oats tend to produce a wash that is weaker in alcohol than from barley and would therefore need to be redistilled several times. Yet whatever grain was used for distilling meant less grain for food – a critical issue at times.

In the first half of the nineteenth century many Highlanders had been pushed off their land during the Clearances and resettled on the islands and along the West Coast. With tiny strips to cultivate in the infertile soil it was real subsistence farming and when the potato crop failed, as it did spectacularly in the 1840s, it caused famine. Plenty gave up the struggle and emigrated to the New World or moved to join one of the surging industries down south. In Glasgow so many used to gather under the great railway arch by Glasgow's Central Station over Argyll Street, to shelter from the weather, that it became known as the "Hielanman's Umbrella".

If the first excise officer only arrived on Islay in 1797, illicit distillers in the Outer Hebrides had little to fear, and apparently those on Lewis were openly distilling away until 1827. By that stage most

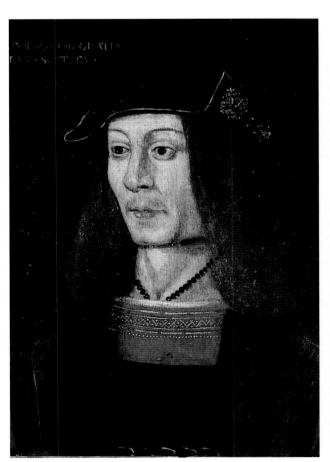

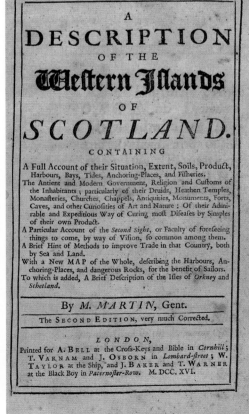

LEFT Martin Martin's travels round the Hebrides, *A Description of the Western Islands of Scotland*, published in 1703, includes a fascinating early account of whisky and its popularity among the islanders.

FAR LEFT James IV of Scotland, one of the more successful Stuart monarchs. His Statutes of Iona of 1609 included an attempt to curb the flow of "strong wines and acquavitie" through the Western Isles.

mainland distillers had taken out licences as the industry came of age. Before long, being out on some remote island became a serious disadvantage to anyone making whisky. Malt distilleries were an anonymous link in the supply chain, and if you were out on Tiree or South Uist your costs were bound to be considerably higher than for distillers on the mainland.

Finally, with the modern era of single malts provenance has become highly important, and there is an obvious benefit from being able to boast that you are the only distillery on a particular island. First of the new generation of offshore distillers was Harold Currie, who founded Arran in 1995, almost 160 years since the island's last licensed distillery closed. Arran trades on its strong connection with Robert Burns, and is the only whisky allowed to use the bard's image and signature on its label.

Up on Lewis, Mark Tayburn founded the Abhainn Dearg distillery, and in 2010 was able to export the island's first cask of whisky for 170 years, while five years later the stills of the nearby Isle of Harris distillery were fired into life. Harris calls itself a social distillery with everything distilled, matured and bottled on the island to create the maximum

employment. "The population of Harris has halved in the last 50 years as the young migrate to the mainland," says the distillery's MD, Simon Erlanger. "So you've got an ageing population and a very fragile economy."

LEFT A fresh consignment of empty casks for filling at the Arran distillery.

OPPOSITE Abhainn Dearg (pronounced "aveen jarrek") distillery in Uig on the Isle of Harris. It was founded in 2010 on the site of an abandoned fish farm in 2010, with a pair of converted hot water tanks for stills.

BELOW Kenny Maclean, production manager at the new isle of Harris distillery in Tarbert, with some of the locals.

TALISKER
CARBOST, ISLE OF SKYE, INVERNESS-SHIRE

FROM A DISTANCE THIS COMPACT, WHITEWASHED DISTILLERY LOOKS SMALL AND RATHER INSIGNIFICANT BENEATH THE CUILLIN HILLS WITH THEIR BLACK GRANITE FACE AND JAGGED RIDGE SLIPPING IN AND OUT OF THE CLOUDS. YET IF THE BUILDINGS ARE OVERSHADOWED, AT LEAST THE WHISKIES PRODUCED HERE HAVE THE POWER, DEPTH AND COMPLEXITY TO REFLECT THE DRAMA OF THE LANDSCAPE.

The story of Talisker begins in 1825 when brothers Hugh and Kenneth MacAskill took out a lease, on the Talisker House estate, where Johnson and Boswell had stayed on their Hebridean tour in the 1760s. By this time the local industry of harvesting kelp from the sea shore to turn into soap and glass was in decline, and people were emigrating to the New World. The MacAskills helped them on their way by replacing the crofters with Cheviot sheep.

After an aborted attempt to site a distillery five miles north at Fiskavaig, they settled on the hamlet of Carbost and spent £3,000 building Talisker in 1830. The name came from the feature known as *Talamh Sgeir* or "Echo Rock" that stood on the shore. The local minister was passionately opposed and described the distillery's impact on his parish as "one of the greatest curses which, in the ordinary course of Providence, could befall it". In 1848 his prayers were answered when the venture was

acquired by the North of Scotland Bank for a third of the amount it had cost to build. Two other licensees tried and failed to make a go of Talisker before Roderick Kemp and Alexander Grigor Allan took over in 1876.

Kemp was an entrepreneur from Aberdeen, while his partner was involved with the Dailuaine distillery on Speyside. Business soon picked up, as was clear from the regular coming and going of small steamers, or "puffers", arriving with grain and leaving laden with whisky. Unfortunately, the lack of a pier meant the casks had to be set afloat and towed three or four hundred yards out into the loch to be winched aboard. Despite increasingly desperate letters to the laird, Macleod of Dunvegan, the pier was only built in 1900. But Kemp had long since given up on Skye, selling out to his partner in 1892 and moving to the other side of Scotland where he bought Macallan.

BELOW LEFT The MacAskill brothers were tenant farmers on Skye who played a small part in the Highland clearances by evicting crofters on their land, and replacing them with more profitable sheep. Whisky was just one of the business ventures they tried.

BELOW The functional, whitewashed buildings of Talisker are dwarfed by the distillery's dramatic setting, but its whisky is sufficiently robust and fiery to have been dubbed "the lava of the Cuillins".

OPPOSITE Today the far-flung beauty of Skye is an asset to the island's only single malt whisky, but in the days when almost every drop of Talisker disappeared into blends, its remoteness must have made the distillery feel quite vulnerable at times.

HUGH MACASKILL, OF RHUANDUNAN AND TALISKER (1799-1863).

SAVED BY THE FIRE

For Robert Louis Stevenson it was a grand whisky – "The King o' drinks, as I conceive it, Talisker, Islay or Glenlivet!" Soon after that endorsement Talisker teamed up with Dailuaine, whose major shareholder was Talisker's manager, Thomas Mackenzie. The pair of distilleries was gradually acquired by the Distillers Company (DCL), who gained full control in 1925. Unlike most of its rivals, some Talisker was already being sold as a single malt, though most was being used in blends. It became a key filling in Johnnie Walker and had the brand's famous striding man logo on the label of its malts until the 1980s. This connection may have just tipped the balance when DCL accountants questioned the wisdom of keeping going such a far-flung distillery with all its added transport costs. Unlike Islay there were no sister distilleries on Skye to share the expense, and the bridge to the mainland was not built until 1995.

Some claim it was the fire in 1960, when spirit leaked out of one of the spirits stills and set the whole building ablaze, that saved Talisker. Having invested so much in the new still-house, its owners could not bear to close it down for good in the 1980s when the industry was drowning in surplus whisky. Yet probably more important was its inclusion in the original six Classic Malts in 1988. Its renown as a single malt took a while to catch on, but today it is hard to imagine that the distillery, which attracts over 50,000 visitors in a good year, was ever in danger.

One of the curiosities about Talisker is that it was originally triple distilled like an Irish whiskey. Today it has three wash stills supplying a pair of spirit stills and the strangest set of lyne arms in the whole of Scotland. These are the copper pipes that connect the neck of the still to the condensers, or old-fashioned worm tubs in the case of Talisker, where the vapours are condensed into spirit. Instead of being straight, as at most distilleries, the lyne arms are contorted into a giant U shape which is connected to the still via something called a reflux pipe. Apparently up to 90 per cent of the vapour condenses back down this pipe to be redistilled.

Maybe the reason for this weird configuration was an attempt to replicate the old triple-distilled taste of Talisker, but no one really knows. What is true is that the cleansing effect of the extra copper contact that strips out impurities is offset by the inherent smokiness of the malt and the use of worm tubs, which tend to produce a heavier spirit. It all goes to make Talisker a truly unique single malt, and no one would dare tamper with any part of the production process. Its owners, Diageo, produce a range of ages, including the standard 10-year-old and the highly rated 18-year-old, of which all but one are bottled at 45.8 per cent abv. As with other popular single malts, growing demand has squeezed the supply of aged stocks and in response the distillery has released various expressions without age-statements like the recent Talisker Storm.

WHISKY TASTING NOTES
TALISKER STORM 45.8% ABV

Talisker has been bringing out a host of new expressions without age-statements, which might concern lovers of the superb 18-year-old, which has become harder to find, but there is nothing to worry about with Storm. The name pays tribute to Talisker's rugged location on the western side of Skye beside Loch Harport where things can get pretty stormy.

There is plenty of spice on the nose, ginger, and Talisker's signature peppery note with a thread of smoke. On the tongue this is a dense, richly textured dram with pronounced sweetness at first. On the back of the tongue comes the heat of the pepper as the peaty flavours come through. Adding water seems to underline the whisky's slightly salty edge.

TOBERMORY

TOBERMORY, ISLE OF MULL, ARGYLL & BUTE

MULL'S CAPITAL TOBERMORY, WITH ITS PRETTY SEAFRONT OF BRIGHTLY COLOURED HOUSES, WAS ESTABLISHED IN 1788 AS A MODEL VILLAGE BY THE BRITISH SOCIETY FOR PROMOTING THE FISHERIES. NINE YEARS LATER JOHN SINCLAIR, A LOCAL KELP MERCHANT, PROPOSED A DISTILLERY, BUT THE AUTHORITIES SUGGESTED HE BUILD A BREWERY INSTEAD. WHETHER HE SIMPLY IGNORED THEM OR WAITED UNTIL 1823 WHEN THE DISTILLERY WAS OFFICIALLY REGISTERED IS UNCLEAR. EITHER WAY TOBERMORY'S CURRENT OWNERS INSIST IT BEGAN MAKING WHISKY IN 1798, MAKING IT ONE OF THE OLDEST COMMERCIAL DISTILLERIES IN SCOTLAND STILL GOING. THE DATE IS EMBOSSED ON EVERY BOTTLE OF SINGLE MALT.

Sinclair leased a small area of land by the coast called Ledaig – Gaelic for "safe haven". In his first year he produced a paltry 292 gallons of spirit, possibly because he was still officially a brewer, or maybe because of his other business interests. He had a small fleet of vessels to ferry the kelp to Glasgow and Liverpool where it was used to make soap and glass. When he died in 1837, the distillery died with him in the first of many long siestas. In the words of Alan McConnochie, the former distillery manager: "Tobermory may have suffered from being run by enthusiastic amateurs."

Thirty years later in was back in production and, after a string of owners, passed to the Distillers Co. in 1916. It was a brief interlude however, for in June 1930 during the Depression, Tobermory shut down and remained so for 41 years. At first it would have been "mothballed" for better times ahead, but once the stills and washbacks had been ripped out, the likelihood of it ever making whisky again faded with each passing year.

In 1971, a consortium of "enthusiastic amateurs"

BELOW Tobermory's stills, which were shut down in 2017 so they could be replaced, produced two distinct whiskies – the peated Ledaig single malt and Tobermory itself.

performed an extraordinary act of resuscitation on Tobermory. Maybe they were seduced by its dreamy setting cradled beneath high cliffs across the bay from Scotland's most photographed waterfront. Or perhaps it was the size of the development grant. The venture soon failed, but by putting in new stills and washbacks and restoring the building, it was enough to rescue the distillery which was bought by Burn Stewart in 1993. With the burgeoning interest in single malts, especially from Islay, Tobermory's relatively remote island location suddenly became its core strength. And now with over two decades of uninterrupted production there are sufficient stocks for a raft of aged expressions either as "Tobermory", or its peated cousin – "Ledaig".

In 2013 Tobermory was purchased along with its sister distilleries of Deanston and Bunnahabhain, by the South African group – Distell. In early 2017 it was announced that whisky production would stop for two years while a new set of stills were installed.

RIGHT Tobermory's flagship 10-year-old and its sister malt – Ledaig – are fairly recent creations. For most of its history the distillery was at the whim of the big blenders, and spent much of the twentieth century in mothballs.

WHISKY TASTING NOTES
LEDAIG 10-YEAR-OLD 46.3% ABV

Since it went back into full-time production after decades lying idle, the Tobermory distillery has had a split personality. It all revolves around peat, which is barely present in the eponymous single malt, but wafts out of its sister malt – Ledaig – pronounced Led-chig. Both whiskies have doubtless benefited from being bottled at a higher strength without the need to chill filter. With Ledaig the smoke is gentle and soft and perhaps more evident on the tongue than the nose, where there is also a vague hint of pine. In the mouth there is a definite malty richness that also comes from the wood, cut with some spicy flavours, possibly cloves and black pepper. There is a smoky mineral note on the finish.

ON THE WHISKY TRAIL

TOBERMORY

LEFT With its natural harbour, Tobermory was an ideal location for a new fishing village in 1788. Today its brightly coloured seafront has been popularized by the children's television series *Balamory*.

JURA
ISLE OF JURA, ARGYLL & BUTE

TO THE SOUTH, JUTTING OUT FROM THE EASTERN EDGE OF ISLAY, IS JURA WHOSE TINY POPULATION WAS ONCE ALLOWED TO DISTIL WHISKY FOR ITS OWN CONSUMPTION UNTIL IT WAS BANNED IN 1781. SOME THIRTY YEARS LATER A CERTAIN ARCHIBALD CAMPBELL ESTABLISHED A DISTILLERY ON THE WATERFRONT AT CRAIGHOUSE IN THE SOUTH OF THE ISLAND. IT IMPRESSED ALFRED BARNARD WHEN HE VISITED IN THE MID-1880S. HE DECLARED ISLE OF JURA TO BE "ONE OF THE HANDSOMEST WE HAVE SEEN, AND FROM THE BAY LOOKS MORE LIKE A CASTLE THAN A DISTILLERY".

In 1901 after a dispute with Colin Campbell, the landowner, the distillery's then owner – James Ferguson – proceeded to dismantle it. The island ran dry of its own whisky until 1963 when two estate owners teamed up with the whisky blenders Charles Mackinlay & Co., to build a new Isle of Jura distillery. Part of their intention was to create some much-needed full-time jobs on the island.

They hired the architect William Delmé-Evans who had previously designed and been one of the founders of the Perthshire distillery – Tullibardine in 1949. Delmé-Evans was also later involved in Glenallachie up by the Moray Firth, but he clearly had a special bond with Isle of Jura, becoming managing

director of the distillery until he retired in 1975. A decade later Mackinlay & Co. which was effectively the whisky division of Scottish & Newcastle Breweries, was bought by Invergordon distillers, who in turn were gobbled up by Whyte & Mackay.

It is fair to say Isle of Jura was somewhat neglected as a single malt, as its new owners focused on their Whyte & Mackay blend, on supplying supermarket own-label Scotch and on fighting off much bigger competitors like Diageo.

When it came to single malts, their pride and joy was clearly Dalmore. Yet in 2007, when Whyte & Mackay itself was bought up by the Indian drinks giant "United Spirits" the new boss Vijay Malya

BELOW Jutting out from the eastern flank of Islay, there is a wild remoteness to Jura where the red deer outnumber the inhabitants 30:1. It was here that George Orwell escaped to write his great dystopian novel, *Nineteen Eighty-Four.*

declared that Jura had always been his father's favourite whisky.

The old labels depicting the Island of Jura alone on a sea with no sign of Islay, were dropped, and the bottle given a new curvaceous waistline. New expressions appeared led by Superstition, one of the first mainstream malts not to carry an age-statement.

There are now a series of aged expressions ranging from the 10-year-old Origin to the 30-year-old Camas an Staca which spends its last three years maturing in sherry butts.

WHISKY TASTING NOTES
ISLE OF JURA PROPHECY 46% ABV

The eye on the label of this limited release malt refers to an eighteenth-century soothsayer who foretold that the last of the Campbell clan would leave the island with one eye and with all his worldly possessions in a cart pulled by a white horse. And that is exactly what happened in 1938, the eye being lost in the First World War. Taste for yourself whether the whisky will be such a legend, but there is plenty going on with its beach bonfire nose and spicy nutmeg aromas. On the tongue the smoke dominates until richer, more spicy notes emerge. According to Richard Patterson, the man who crafted the whisky, there are also traces of damp moss and Arbroath smokies.

ABOVE Casks waiting to be shipped across the Sound of Islay to Jura.

LEFT The Jura Distillery was designed by William Delmé-Evans and opened in 1963 He later became the distillery's managing director.

THE HIGHLANDS

"THE WHISKY OF THIS COUNTY," WROTE ROBERT BURNS, "IS A MOST RASCALLY LIQUOR, AND BY CONSEQUENCE, ONLY DRUNK BY THE MOST RASCALLY PART OF THE INHABITANTS." HIS WORDS, IN A LETTER TO AN AYRSHIRE FRIEND, DATE FROM A TIME WHEN SCOTLAND PRODUCED TWO VERY DIFFERENT TYPES OF WHISKY. THERE WAS THE LEGALIZED STUFF PRODUCED BY LICENSED DISTILLERS IN THE LOWLANDS, AND THE ILLICIT VARIETY MOST ASSOCIATED WITH THE HIGHLANDS. BURNS WAS ALMOST CERTAINLY REFERRING TO THE FORMER, WHICH WAS PUMPED OUT ON AN INDUSTRIAL SCALE IN LARGE, SHALLOW-BOTTOMED STILLS AT A FEARSOME PACE. UP IN THE HIGHLANDS, WHICH HAD YET TO EMBRACE THE INDUSTRIAL REVOLUTION IN ANY FORM, SOMETHING LESS "RASCALLY" WOULD HAVE BEEN PRODUCED.

THE WHISKY HERITAGE OF THE HIGHLANDS

IF HIGHLAND AND LOWLAND WHISKY OPERATED AT DIFFERENT SPEEDS IT WAS PARTLY THE FAULT OF THE WASH ACT OF 1784. THIS SET THE SIZE OF THE LICENCE FEE ACCORDING TO THE CAPACITY OF THE DISTILLERY AND THUS ENCOURAGED THE BIG LOWLAND DISTILLERS IN THEIR PURSUIT OF VOLUME. FOR THEM THE BIG MARKET WAS NOT SO MUCH WHISKY DRINKERS IN SCOTLAND AS THE GIN-SOAKED CITIZENS OF LONDON. MOST OF THE RAW SPIRIT THEY PRODUCED WAS SENT SOUTH FOR RECTIFYING INTO ENGLISH GIN. RECOGNIZING THAT CONDITIONS WERE TOUGHER IN THE NORTH, THE ACT ALLOWED ANYONE DISTILLING THERE, NORTH OF A LINE THAT RAN LOOSELY FROM DUNOON TO DUNDEE, TO USE SMALLER STILLS. IT ALSO EXEMPTED THEM FROM THE DREADED MALT TAX. TO PLACATE THE LOWLAND DISTILLERS, WHO FEARED UNFAIR COMPETITION, IT WAS DECREED THAT NO HIGHLAND WHISKY WAS TO CROSS THE LINE.

So was born the idea of the Highlands as a whisky region, and the belief that its whiskies were better for being distilled in small pot stills at a slower pace than in the industrial distilleries to the south. That was no doubt true up to a point, and as the authorities spread northwards in their campaign to stamp out the production of moonshine and smuggling, illicit Highland whisky began to flow south. Being illegal somehow made it taste all the sweeter. As the Irish said of poteen, it was "superior in sweetness, salubriety and gusto to all that machinery, science and capital can produce in the legalized way".

LEFT The use of peat to fire the kilns that dried the malt in Highland distilleries was no calculated decision as often it would have been the only fuel available. As a result most whiskies would have been considerably more smoky than today.

THE SPIRIT OF DEFIANCE

There was also a political dimension. Having crushed the Jacobites at the battle of Culloden in 1746, the government was determined to bring the whole of Scotland firmly to heel. Among a range of measures the wearing of kilts and the playing of bagpipes were no longer permitted. Denied their national dress or music, it was no wonder people took to whisky as the spirit of defiance. One should not get too misty-eyed, however. The quality would have been extremely variable and the taste would have been raw and harsh without the softening effect of a slow maturation in wood, or at least some added herbs and sugar.

The geographic fault line that splits the country in two, from the shores of Loch Lomond to the south Aberdeenshire coast, can be seen from space, while the Highlands themselves were once as tall as the Himalayas. As the Lowlands embraced the industrial revolution, the Highlands slipped backwards – a twilight zone compared to that beacon of the Enlightenment, Edinburgh.

Yet in the early nineteenth century the Highlands were rebranded as a tragic and romantic dreamscape by Sir Walter Scott, whose epic poem *The Lady of the Lake* effectively launched the Scottish tourist industry. Before long Victorians were flocking to see Scott's "land of the mountain and the flood" for themselves, while the locals were heading in the opposite direction. There was the lure of employment in the factories, mills and shipyards of the Central Belt and, for some, the threat of eviction in favour of sheep during the Highland clearances.

The romance of the Highlands was firmly embraced by the Scotch whisky industry as illicit farm distilleries in remote glens came in from the cold and took out licences in the 1820s. The Central Highlands – being the broad sweep of land from Loch Lomond to Perth via the Ochills and the Campsie Fells – was home to almost 130 licensed distilleries. The area was probably producing more

BELOW Without water there would be no *aqua vitae*, or water of life, but a shortage of rain to top up the burns and lochs has seldom been an issue in the Highlands.

BELOW LEFT Teacher's Highland Cream was a popular, well-established brand of Scotch by the time this advertising poster appeared in 1904. Note the bearded Scotsman from central casting in the back.

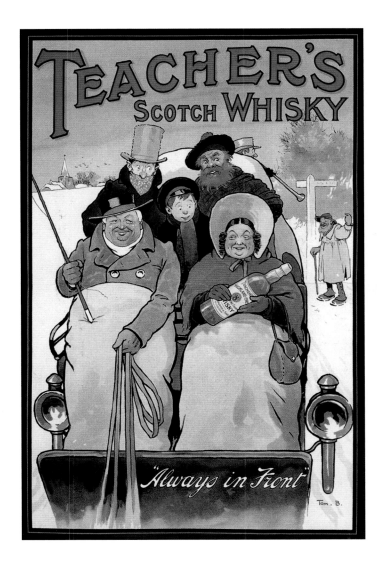

malt whisky than anywhere else in Scotland if you include all the moonshine that was still being made well into the nineteenth century. The smugglers enjoyed a good passing trade along the old drove routes that connected upland grazing with the big Lowland cattle markets.

A HIGHLAND CULL

Today there are just five distilleries in the region, mainly clustered towards Perth. The city had a long tradition in the drinks trade through wine, and later became a major hub of the Victorian railways. Before long it was home to whisky blenders like Dewar's, Bell's and Matthew Gloag & Sons of The Famous Grouse. Sometimes the blends came first, as in Dewar's White Label, whose success prompted the firm to build the Aberfeldy distillery in 1896.

Over in the Western Highlands the cull of old distilleries was even more dramatic, with just two survivors in Oban and Ben Nevis on the mainland, and another two beyond if you include Talisker on Skye and Tobermory on Mull. Being in Fort William, an important garrison town, must have helped Ben Nevis, while Oban was popular as "the gateway to the Isles", and both benefited from being on the railways. As for the rest that have disappeared, many were simply too small to survive once local demand evaporated along with a declining population. The big blending houses in cities like Glasgow had easier

access to malt whisky from elsewhere.

Over on the East Coast there were over 70 distilleries built in Angus and Aberdeenshire, but despite plentiful supplies of the best barley in Scotland, only a tiny handful have survived. Aberdeen and Inverness were once thriving whisky towns, but their distilleries have all gone, buried beneath flats and supermarkets. Distilling has fared better beyond Inverness where there are nine distilleries still going, including two on Orkney.

Given the sheer scale of the Highlands, not many distilleries are excluded. Even Campbeltown's Springbank is technically in the Highlands, even though it is further south than Berwick upon Tweed. Glengoyne, 14 miles north of Glasgow, just squeezes over the line and is thus as much a Highland whisky as Pulteney in Wick – a good five hours away by car. The brisk, maritime whiskies of the West Coast are closer to the sweet, cereal Perthshire malts in terms of where they are distilled, but far removed when it comes to style. All this goes to show that the term "Highland" is not much of a signpost to help novice whisky drinkers into the single malt jungle.

BELOW Point of sale material included everything from ceramic figures and decanters to ash trays and drip mats like this pair from Buchanan's which for decades was run a separate fiefdom within DCL.

ABOVE Old Pulteney in Wick, Caithness, can trace its distilling roots back to 1826 and its various brands have been regular award-winners.

LEFT The lauter tun has become a familiar sight in malt distilleries across Scotland. The process involves sparging, whereby the grist is sprayed with hot water to extract as much of its soluble sugar as possible. The draff left behind is used as cattle feed.

GLENMORANGIE
TAIN, ROSS-SHIRE

GLENMORANGIE'S STILLS ARE MORE FEMININE THAN THE DUMPY, ONION-SHAPED ONES YOU FIND IN MOST DISTILLERIES AND, AT NEARLY 17 FEET, THEIR SLENDER NECKS ARE THE TALLEST IN THE INDUSTRY. GLENMORANGIE NOW HAS 12 OF THEM, APPARENTLY ALL MODELLED ON THE PAIR OF SECOND-HAND GIN STILLS FROM LONDON BOUGHT BY WILLIAM MATHESON WHEN HE FIRST OBTAINED A LICENCE TO DISTIL WHISKY ON HIS FARM IN 1843. THE DISTILLERY GREW OUT OF AN OLD BREWERY THAT HE INHERITED WHEN HE TOOK OUT A LEASE ON THE MORANGIE FARM NEAR TAIN ON THE SOUTHERN SHORES OF THE DORNOCH FIRTH.

By the time the Victorian whisky writer Alfred Barnard visited 40 years later, Glenmorangie was producing 20,000 gallons a year. This was quite a feat for a distillery that he claimed was "almost in ruins", and "certainly the most ancient and primitive" he had seen. One suspects Barnard was doubtful the distillery would survive, which it has in spectacular fashion. Had he been able to travel through time and revisit the distillery today he would be amazed. His eyes would doubtless bulge at the sheer scale of the place, which hums with a relentless rhythm 24 hours a day, seven days a week – and would probably pop out of their sockets at the sight of the computer screen through which the entire distillation process is controlled by one man.

All this was way into the future, and would never have happened without the late-nineteenth-century boom in blended Scotch. This brought outside investment into the Glenmorangie Distillery Co. formed in 1887, and allowed the distillery's complete renovation before it collapsed altogether. Yet interestingly not all the whisky was sold to the blenders, for casks of its "pure Highland Malt" were being shipped as far as San Francisco. On seeing a consignment destined for Rome, the local paper speculated whether the Pope himself had requested "the Mountain Dew of Easter Ross", as it daintily referred to the whisky.

Production doubled after the rebuilding, and the distillery clung on through the boom-bust years at the start of the twentieth century. It limped through the

LEFT A sea of American oak bourbon barrels waiting to be filled with Glenmorangie's sweet new-make spirit. After ten years most of the whisky will be bottled, but some will be sent to "finishing school" for a matter of months, or even years, in a more exotic cask.

OPPOSITE At just under 17 feet high, these are the tallest pot stills in the industry. Allegedly, each one is modelled on the original pair bought second-hand from a Victorian gin distillery by Glenmorangie's founder, William Matheson.

First World War, when recruits from the Argyll & Sutherland Highlanders were billeted in its malt barns, and was up for sale before the war was over. In April 1918 it was bought by Macdonald & Muir, a leading firm of blenders from Leith, for the princely sum of £74,100.

BLENDS ACROSS THE SEA

New ownership brought security, for Macdonald & Muir had a number of popular blends like Highland Queen to soak up Glenmorangie's production of malt whisky, which was swiftly cranked up to 110,000 gallons a year. The barley mostly came from local farmers and was delivered to the malt barns near the entrance. From there the production process flowed downhill, for the barley to be steeped, then spread over floor maltings for a week and then dried over a peat kiln. Peat was used exclusively until the late 1940s, cut at first from the nearby Tarlogie hills, which have always been the source of Glenmorangie's water, and then from Orkney.

The worldwide slump sparked off by the Wall Street Crash of 1929 led to the distillery shutting down in March 1931 for five years. In the meantime the ending of Prohibition in the USA signalled a light at the end of the tunnel for firms like Macdonald & Muir. By the outbreak of the Second World War, almost four-fifths of all the whisky produced by the company was being shipped to America. Much of the US success was down to the firm's "Martin's VVO" blend, which included a good dollop of Glenmorangie.

By 1971 Americans were drinking 36 million cases of Scotch whisky a year – a threefold increase on 1960. The industry was in rude health and happily extrapolated past sales to predict future growth. Unfortunately, however, its US consumers were ageing and giving Scotch the image of "an old man's drink" among a new generation that had embraced vodka. As US sales slipped into decline, Glenmorangie began to explore other avenues. With William Grant's enjoying success with Glenfiddich, it was decided to start laying down stocks for a regular single malt.

It was a smart move and, by the late 1970s, such was demand for its 10-year-old malt, the company decided to cease floor malting and build a new still-room on the site. Within ten years, Glenmorangie had caught up with its great rival Glenfiddich in the UK, and was soon claiming to be the bestselling single malt in Scotland. The company became a PLC, though it remained in the control of the Macdonald family, and in 1997 bought Ardbeg.

FINISHING SCHOOL

Since the 1920s the firm had also owned Glen Moray on Speyside, but with just three distilleries there was a need to expand the repertoire of its flagship malt – Glenmorangie – to compete with much larger rivals in the market. Dr Bill Lumsden, now the firm's head of distilling and whisky creation, was given the job of innovation to come up with new expressions of the single malt. After a decade maturing in American oak, ex-bourbon barrels, the whisky was either bottled as the 10-year-old, or sent to "finishing school" to spend six months to a year maturing in different casks.

These included a port wood finish, a sherry cask finish and a Sauternes finish, which began to appear alongside the 10-year-old mother hen like a brood of chicks. Glenmorangie's expanded family spread across the supermarket shelves, displacing some of its rival malts completely – a perhaps not unintended consequence. A raft of other finishes came and went as Lumsden and his team pushed the concept to the limit, and while the mania for wood innovation may have subsided, it certainly boosted Glenmorangie's sales.

In 2004 the French luxury goods group Louis Vuitton Moët Hennessy gobbled up Glenmorangie PLC for £300,000 and gave the whiskies a suitably luxurious makeover with prices to match. The bottles became curvaceous and new names were conjured up. Out went the prosaic-sounding port finish, which became "Quinta Ruban", while the Sauternes now glories in the title "Nectar d'Or".

WHISKY TASTING NOTES
GLENMORANGIE NECTAR D'OR 12-YEAR-OLD 46% ABV

If you can forgive the slightly pretentious name, Nectar d'Or is what was once known as the Glenmorangie Sauternes finish, or "extra matured" as they now like to call it. It comes from the standard 10-year-old that is pulled from its slumbers in ex-bourbon American oak barrels to spend up to two years in casks that previously held the famous sweet pudding wine of Bordeaux.

The result is a fabulously seductive, silky-smooth take on Glenmorangie's light, honeyed orange peel style. What comes through from the months at finishing school is probably less to do with the cask's previous contents than the spicy quality of the European oak that complements the coconut sweetness of those old bourbon barrels.

PULTENEY
WICK, CAITHNESS

HUDDLED BESIDE THE NORTH SEA, THE SMALL TOWN OF WICK CAN FEEL PRETTY BLEAK AT TIMES. IT LIES JUST EIGHTEEN MILES SOUTH OF SCOTLAND'S NORTHERN TIP OF JOHN O'GROATS, AND APART FROM DOUNREAY, A FEW LOCAL SERVICES AND SOME INSHORE FISHING THERE IS NOT MUCH WORK TO KEEP HOLD OF THE YOUNG. LIKE OTHER HIGHLAND OUTPOSTS, WICK'S POPULATION IS SHRINKING SLOWLY.

It is hard to believe, therefore, that this was once the great boom town of the north whose size was doubling every decade in the latter half of the nineteenth century. It was all down to the humble herring, for which Wick became the biggest fishing port in Europe – far larger than Hull or Grimsby, with a fleet of up to 1,000 boats. It was said that when they were all in port you could walk from one side of the harbour to the other across the decks, while the assembled masts would have been the closest thing to a forest in this part of Scotland. At the start of the fishing season, an army of workers descended on the harbour to gut the fish and pack them into salt barrels. The barrels were then loaded on to cargo ships to feed the insatiable demand for herring on the other side of the North Sea.

THIRSTY WORK
The harbour was originally part of Pulteneytown,

which faced its neighbour of Wick on the other side of the river. It was a purpose-built fishing village designed by the engineer Thomas Telford in the early 1800s, and commissioned by Sir William Pulteney MP, the first chairman of the British Fisheries Society. With fishing and gutting fish such thirsty work, James Henderson, who had been making whisky at his family home for some time, seized the opportunity with both hands.

He founded Pulteney in 1826 as an urban distillery in the centre of the community with its own captive market. The town's customs officers ensured there was no threat of competition from illicit stills, and there was easy access to other markets along the east coast and over the sea to Russia, Germany and the Baltic States. Not that there was any great need to export, given the scale of demand on the doorstep. According to one report from the 1840s, this modest fishing

BELOW LEFT By appearances Pulteney employed more folk than Glenmorangie and its famous "16 men of Tain" who were also invariably pictured with wooden shovels, known as shiels, used to turn the malt.

BELOW The prominent boil ball connecting the base to the neck of Pulteney's stills inspired the whisky's patented bottle.

village was consuming a staggering 500 gallons (2,230 litres) of whisky per day. It seems Henderson could not have picked a better place.

His two stills were rudimentary and had a curious shape, assuming the current ones are modelled on them. They have a bulbous boil ball, like a huge Adam's apple beneath the neck, which is mimicked by Old Pulteney's bottle. They are hardly the most handsome stills in the whisky industry, and appear to have been sawn off at the neck as though to fit beneath the still-house roof. Today there is ample space for more elegant stills, but no one is thinking of changing the design now.

For as long as anyone can remember the whisky has been known as Old Pulteney, and was once "perfectly white", claimed the novelist Neil Gunn, recalling his childhood in the early twentieth century. It was consumed "on the quays of Wick more for its effect than its flavour", or so he said. If it really was colourless, they were either drinking new-make spirit fresh from the still, or the casks used were totally inactive.

By the outbreak of the First World War, Scotland's herring fleet was already shrinking thanks to the larger Scandinavian drift netters. The backlash against the demon drink had already started, and the town's 10,000-strong, seasonal workforce was blamed for all manner of depravity. In 1920 Henderson's descendants sold the distillery to James Watson & Co., a firm of blenders from Dundee. It was good timing on his part, for in 1922 Wick, along with 56 other towns in Scotland, voted to go dry and remained so for 25 years. It was the high water mark of the temperance movement when Edwin Scrymgeour, Britain's first and last prohibitionist MP, defeated Winston Churchill in Dundee in that year's general election.

SPREADING THE NEWS

A few years later James Watson & Co. was swallowed up by the Distillers Company, who promptly closed the distillery down in 1930. It was not until 1951 that Robert Cumming, a local lawyer who had also acquired Balblair down the coast near Tain, cranked Pulteney back to life. It then passed to the Canadian group Hiram Walker, who effectively rebuilt it in the late 1950s, before they too were absorbed, this time into Allied Distillers. Finally, in 1995 Pulteney came to rest with its present owners Inver House Distillers, who gave this rather neglected, far-flung outpost of Scotch whisky some much-needed TLC.

As long as its malt production disappeared into blended Scotch, Pulteney was acutely vulnerable to the cycles of the whisky industry, particularly given its remoteness. Beyond the town and those in the business, the distillery was anonymous. That changed with the launch of Old Pulteney 12-year-old single malt in 1997 to mark the 50th anniversary of the repeal of prohibition in Wick. Inver House has drawn heavily on the whisky's maritime heritage: the way the barley and barrels were transported by boat and how the distillery workers were often fishermen as well. A fishing boat is etched on the bottle, and the brand has sponsored various seafaring endeavours. These have included Sir Robin Knox-Johnson's successful bid to sail solo round the world for a second time in 2007, and Jock Wishart's expedition to the North Pole by rowing boat four years later.

Inver House also restored an old herring drifter, the *Isabella Fortuna*, to spread the news of what it called "The Genuine Maritime Malt" up and down the coast, and gradually brought out older expressions up to and including a 40-year-old in 2012. There have also been a couple of non-age-statement whiskies named after the *Fortuna* and another herring drifter – *The Good Hope*. All this reflects a whisky that may not actually contain any salt, but does have a trace of sea spray on the nose to complement the sweeter, fruit and nut flavours on the tongue.

BELOW When Wick was a fishing boom town with a fleet of 1,000 boats and a huge seasonal workforce with an insatiable thirst for whisky, its resident distillery could barely keep up with demand.

WHISKY TASTING NOTES
OLD PULTENEY 12-YEAR-OLD 40% ABV

The northernmost distillery on the Scottish mainland does a raft of older single malts and different expressions that play on wood like Navigator – a marriage of sherry and bourbon casks – but its flagship 12-year-old is a cracking whisky and pretty good value too. Swirled around in the glass, there is a pleasing fragrance that combines some tropical notes like bananas with a grassy aroma and maritime freshness. The coastal, far-flung setting of the distillery may well exaggerate the desire to find a salty note, but there is something there. On the tongue there is a gentle citrus fruitiness and notes of orange peel with a little caramel sweetness that gives it a nice, mouth-coating texture. The finish is lingering and dry.

HIGHLAND PARK, SCAPA AND THE DISTILLERIES OF THE NORTH EAST

HIGHLAND PARK ON ORKNEY HAS LONG BEEN THE MOST NORTHERLY OUTPOST OF WHISKY MAKING IN SCOTLAND. AT THE TIME OF WRITING THERE IS A BID TO BUILD A BOUTIQUE DISTILLERY ON SHETLAND, THOUGH PREVIOUS PLANS TO DO SO CAME TO NOTHING. IN THE PAST THERE HAVE BEEN OTHER DISTILLERIES ON ORKNEY, INCLUDING STROMNESS, BUT HIGHLAND PARK AND THE MUCH SMALLER SCAPA ARE ALL THAT SURVIVE.

While the shortage of local grain may have dampened the supply of home-grown whisky, the need for a strong, heart-warming spirit on Orkney has been constant over the centuries, especially during the long, cold winter nights. Come the summer, visitors can bask in equally long hours of sunlight. Guests at the Castel Hotel in Kirkwall, Orkney's capital, used to be offered a dram and a slice of ginger cake whatever hour they arrived.

Highland Park stands just outside Kirkwall and the oldest buildings date from 1826, when Robert Borwick took out the first licence, although it has been claimed the distillery was founded as early as 1798. Illicit distillers were certainly operating in the area, including the local minister, Magnus Eunson, or so it was claimed. According to one story, he escaped being caught with whisky in his church by concealing it inside a coffin. The man who finally arrested him, John Robertson, is said to have taken over the distillery in a brief partnership with Borwick, whose family owned Highland Park until the 1860s. At that point the heir to Highland Park was Robert's youngest son – the Rev. James Borwick who, being a minister of the Kirk, felt compelled to sell the distillery for the princely sum of £450. It then passed through various hands until bought by James Grant, owner of the Glen Grant distillery on Speyside, who doubled the number of stills to four in 1898.

LEFT Highland Park is one of just seven distilleries to have retained its floor maltings for part of its needs. Turning the malt twice a day using a traditional wooden shiel used to cause an ailment known as monkey shoulder.

ABOVE Orkney heather was once used by Highland Park according to the Victorian whisky writer, Alfred Barnard. He wrote that the heather was picked in full bloom in July and laid on the kiln to "impart a delicate flavour of its own to the malt".

HEATHER IS SWEET

By this point some Highland Park was being drunk as a single malt and had even reached the imperial courts of Denmark and Russia, though most was going into blends like Haig's and Ballantine's. The distillery did use a proportion of local "bere" barley – an indigenous, low-yielding strain that disappeared from the mainland, and heather which was laid on top of the peat in the kiln to offset the smoky bitterness. Visitors to the distillery were shown the heather house and then invited to inhale the pronounced sweetness that wafted up from the furnace. That practice died out long ago, and soon the grain was all coming from the mainland. However the distillery is still partly supplied from its own floor maltings and continues to use heathery sweet Orcadian peat, cut from the nearby Hobbister Moor.

By 1937 the value of Highland Park had increased to £185,000 – the price paid by Highland Distillers, which eventually became part of the Edrington Group. Having given its sister distillery Macallan a lavish makeover, they decided to do the same for Highland Park. The packaging was polished up, and a raft of one-offs and limited releases were unleashed to complement the core range of age-statements that begin with the 12-year-old. The

WHISKY TASTING NOTES
HIGHLAND PARK 12-YEAR-OLD 40% ABV

Up on Orkney they have been embracing their Viking roots at Highland Park with expensive, limited-edition whiskies like Odin, Thor and Freya – the Norse Goddess of love. The distillery also does some lovely older whiskies including a gloriously rich and complex 18-year-old. However, the standard 12-year-old sets the bar pretty high with its signature note of heathery peat that adds a real sweetness and sprinkling of spice to this fine dram.

The smoke drifts through to the palate, and adds a pleasing dryness to the richer malty flavours. Yet what you really notice is quite how polished and smooth this whisky tastes. Roll it round your tongue and see if you can pick up some of the dried fruit, peat and spice.

LEFT Overshadowed by its more famous neighbour, Orkney's other distillery on the shores of Scapa bay produces a gently spicy, honeyed 16-year-old single malt

marketing department has relied heavily on the islands' Nordic roots.

Meanwhile, after years on the endangered list, its neighbouring distillery of *Scapa* returned to full production in 2004 after a £2 million refurbishment by Allied Distillers. Without this investment by the distillery's former owners, Scapa would have doubtless disappeared. It was founded in 1885 by the Glasgow blenders Macfarlane & Townsend, and passed to the North American distillers Hiram Walker in 1954. They rebuilt the distillery five years later and installed a Lomond wash still to produce a heavier, more oily spirit. Today the official bottling is the 16-year-old.

MAINLAND MALTS

Back on the mainland, the first distillery after Pulteney is Clynelish, just by the coastal village of Brora, overlooking the Moray Firth. Its functional, box-shaped design dates from 1967 and belies the fact that there was a much older distillery here. The original Clynelish that you can still see was built by a Glasgow blending firm in 1896, replacing an even earlier version that was established by the Marquis

of Stafford in 1819. The new Clynelish may look nothing like the original, but it aimed to produce a similar style of whisky with the same water source and same shaped stills. In 1969 the original distillery was fired up again under the name Brora, though a totally new malt whisky was created. Robust and heavily peated, it was a mainland version of Islay whisky which the distillery's owners needed for its blends. Heading south along the Dornoch Firth, near Glenmorangie, is Balblair, which was established in 1790 by John Ross. The distillery remained in family hands until it was sold to an Inverness wine merchant, Alexander Cowan, in 1894. The following year he rebuilt Balblair half a mile north beside the Highland railway line. By the outbreak of the First World War, Balblair had closed down and remained so until 1949, having been bought by a local solicitor, Robert Cumming, for £48,000 the year before. Then after a couple of decades with Allied Distillers, it was bought by Inver House in 1996. Despite having a whisky known only to blenders and an inventory full of holes, the new owners have carefully built up a reputation for Balblair as a single malt. Like

ABOVE The mothballed distillery of Brora sits in the grounds of modern Clyenlish that was built in 1968. The two were run in tandem until Brora closed in 1983.

WHISKY TASTING NOTES
DALMORE 18-YEAR-OLD 43% ABV

Heavily sherried whiskies divide opinion – some love their sumptuous fruitcake character and almost decadent sweetness, others find them too much as though the wood has swamped the underlying distillery character. But if you lean to the first camp you should give this beauty a try – it has dried fruit, chocolate and cinnamon spice in abundance. The whisky spends 12 years in American oak barrels and then three in Matusalem sherry butts, which infuses the spirit with a resinous nutty flavour. Yet for all its indulgent sherried character, Dalmore 18-year-old is a well-balanced dram, a real winter warmer to be sipped by a log fire after dinner. If not a meal in itself, it is certainly pudding.

Glenrothes, which may well have been the inspiration, the malts are sold in bulbous bottles by vintage stretching back to 1965. On the Black Isle near Inverness, Glen Ord is the sole survivor of a thriving cottage industry of farm distilleries. It was founded in 1838 by Robert Johnstone and Donald MacLennan, who went bankrupt within a decade. Various new owners took it on, until it passed to a firm of blenders in Dundee and finally to the Distillers Company (now Diageo).

The distillery is dwarfed by the neighbouring Glen Ord Maltings, which supply a fair number of local distilleries, but since 2007 it has built a loyal following for the Singleton of Glen Ord single malt in Asia.

ABOVE The Balblair distillery was relocated in 1895 to be beside the Highland railway that opened 33 years earlier.

RIGHT Scotland's east coast from the Black Isle to Berwick-upon-Tweed has always been prime barley country.

DALWHINNIE
DALWHINNIE, INVERNESS-SHIRE

PHOTOGRAPHS OF DALWHINNIE OFTEN SHOW THE DISTILLERY CAKED IN SNOW ABOVE A CAPTION DECLARING IT TO BE "THE HEIGHT OF PERFECTION". AT 1,037 FEET, IT WAS SCOTLAND'S HIGHEST DISTILLERY UNTIL BRAEVAL ON SPEYSIDE CAME IN AT ABOUT 130FT HIGHER, BUT IT REMAINS THE COLDEST PLACE TO MAKE SCOTCH WHISKY WITH A MEAN ANNUAL TEMPERATURE OF JUST 6C. IT WAS FOUNDED AS THE STRATHSPEY DISTILLERY IN 1897 BY JOHN GRANT, ALEX MACKENZIE AND GEORGE SILLAR, THREE LOCAL MEN FROM KINGUSSIE AND GRANTOWN-ON-SPEY.

The romantic reason they picked this windswept bowl in the Central Highlands, was access to soft spring water that collects in the *Lochan an Doire-uaine* 2,000 feet up in the Drumochter hills. The more prosaic answer was access to the Highland railway to bring in supplies of grain and fuel and the empty casks, and to take away the whisky. The first spirit flowed in the spring of 1898 at the height of the speculative boom when the amount of whisky being produced in Scotland bore absolutely no relation to amount being drunk. When the inevitable crash came, the Strathspey distillery was put up for sale.

The new owner, a blender from Leith, apparently bought it for his son. He re-christened it Dalwhinnie and hired the celebrated distillery architect, Charles Doig, to make "considerable improvements" before selling out to Cooke & Bernheimer, the biggest distillers in America for £1,250 in 1905.

This was the first direct American involvement in whisky, beyond just drinking the stuff, and some in the industry feared it might be the start of US take-over. As if to compound such fears, Cooke & Berheimer, immediately hoisted the Stars and Stripes above their massive warehouse in Leith where Scotch whiskies

BELOW A bright autumn day at Dalwhinnie, Scotland's coldest distillery.

were blended "to suit the American palate".

But as things turned out US prohibition intervened in 1919 and Dalwhinnie slipped back into Scottish hands and the well-known blenders Macdonald Greenlees of Leith who were in turn swallowed up by the Distillers Co. in 1926. Twelve years later it was licensed to James Buchanan & Co. as a key filling in their "Black & White" blend with its famous Scottie dogs logo. The distillery's dark slate roves and gleaming, whitewashed walls, are an obvious visual pun on the name.

For much of the twentieth century the "Great North Road" ran past the door, until Dalwhinnie was bypassed by the A9 in the 1970s. The distillery would have had its own community of workers and their families clustered around it, and when it suffered a bad fire in 1934, it was still being powered by steam engines as there was no electricity here or in the village. Without telephones or modern snow ploughs it would have had to have been a pretty self-sufficient operation especially in the pit of winter when it was sometimes cut off by snow.

Because it was built facing the railway line to which it was connected with its own siding, Dalwhinnie now appears rather back-to-front. As a result the first thing you notice, are a pair of raised up, wooden worm tubs steaming away in the outside air. The fact they now enjoy pride of place is just as it should be, since using an old-fashioned copper worm as opposed to a modern condenser helps capture the essence of Dalwhininie. Another factor contributing to the heaviness of the spirit is the pair of large, broad-necked stills.

Despite being the spiritual home of Black & White, Dalwhinnie must have felt a little vulnerable in the 1980s when distilleries began closing to drain the whisky loch. But it was given a boost by its bosses at UDV (now Diageo) when the Dalwhinnie 15-year-old single malt was picked to represent the Highlands among the six Classic Malts that were launched in 1988. A visitors' centre was opened in 1991 just before the distillery closed for three years for a £3.2 million refurbishment.

WHISKY TASTING NOTES
DALWHINNIE 15-YEAR-OLD 43% ABV

There has always been a strong, sulphury element to the new make spirit at Dalwhinnie that flows off the worm tubs. In 1986 these were removed and replaced with modern condensers, but nine years later the worm tubs were back to restore Dalwhinnie's character. This probably explains the need for a long maturation in refill casks. The 15-year-old emerges with a dry, aromatic nose and a smooth-textured heather honey flavour. The finish is generous, drying to a slightly smoky note. It has been described as "a perfect beginner's malt".

TOP Dalwhinnie's tall, swan-necked stills poking through the roof to the worm tubs outside.

RIGHT Fresh snow can hang around for weeks at 1,000 feet in the heart of the Highlands.

ROYAL LOCHNAGAR
CRATHIE, BALLATER, ABERDEENSHIRE

THIS SMALL, WONDERFULLY DISCREET DISTILLERY IS TUCKED AWAY OFF THE MAIN ROAD WHICH FOLLOWS THE NORTH SIDE OF THE RIVER DEE ALL THE WAY TO THE SEA. COMING FROM THE WEST YOU DRIVE PAST ROWS OF SCOTCH PINES — THE REMNANTS OF THE GREAT CALEDONIAN FOREST — BEFORE TURNING SOUTH AT CRATHIE AS IF VISITING BALMORAL. WITH THE QUEEN JUST A MILE AWAY, ROYAL LOCHNAGAR IS AT THE EPICENTRE OF "ROYAL DEESIDE" — A CONCEPT THAT THE TOURIST BOARD CHIEFS AND ESTATE AGENTS HAVE EXTENDED RIGHT DOWN THE VALLEY AS FAR AS THE SUBURBS OF ABERDEEN.

The first distillery in the parish of Crathie was set up in 1825 on the north bank of the river by James Robertson a former smuggler who had decided to go straight. Unfortunately it was burnt down some years later, in an arson attack by another smuggler who clearly didn't welcome the competition. What remained was washed away by a great spate the following year.

The next incarnation was on the south-side of the river, set up by the John Begg's firm of Begg & Buyers in 1845 as the New Lochnagar distillery. The name comes from the 3,800-foot peek of the same name that the poet Byron described as the "most sublime and picturesque amongst our Caledonian Alps".

Byron had stayed here as a boy when recovering from scarlet fever.

It was an ideal setting for a distillery. There was no shortage of water for cooling worms and mixing with the mash. This flowed from a mountain spring down a series of burns to collect behind the Cragnagall dam where it formed a reservoir. There were peats to be had from nearby moors and good quality barley from the distillery's own farm. And to consume the spent grains there were a hundred head of cattle.

Three years after it was built Queen Victoria and Prince Albert moved into Balmoral next-door and after an invitation from Begg, decided to call on the distillery the next day. Within weeks a Royal warrant

BELOW Looking over a drystone wall to the most boutique and well-preserved of Diageo's many distilleries, Royal Lochnagar, close to Balmoral.

was issued and soon after the distillery was calling itself Royal Lochnagar. As well as keeping Balmoral's decanters topped up, there was also John Brown's hip flask. The Queen's man-servant who became her loyal companion after Albert's death, provoked no end of gossip at Court. On one occasion Brown was so "drink taken" he fell flat on his face, at which point the Queen instantly announced that she too had felt the earth move, or so it was said.

But Royal Lochanagar's main role was in supplying Begg's own blends and others like Vat 69, made by his friend William Sanderson in Leith. The distillery was rebuilt in 1906 and with its granite walls, three storey warehouse and solitary pair of stills, has changed little since then. It was acquired by John Dewar & Sons in 1916 and nine years later passed to the Distillers Company which eventually morphed into Diageo. Today it is the smallest in the firm's portfolio of around thirty distilleries with an annual capacity of just 430,000 litres of pure alcohol.

In the dark days of distillery closures in the 1980s Royal Lochnagar must have felt vulnerable being so small and so far from other distilleries. But a decade later it was given a £2 million facelift and became host to Diageo's Malt Advocates course where global employees enjoy a week's total immersion in malt whisky. The spirit produced here is relatively robust despite a slow distillation with lots of copper contact,

and this make it well suited to sherry maturation leading to some rich, buttery notes in the whisky be it as a single malt or in blends such as Johnnie Walker Blue Label and Windsor. Its current range includes a 12 year-old, a heavily sherried Select Reserve and one finished in Moscatel casks.

WHISKY TASTING NOTES
ROYAL LOCHNAGAR 12-YEAR-OLD 43% ABV

With such a limited production, and given the demands of the blends it features in, there are only two permanent single malts on offer – the 12-year-old and the Select Reserve. Being such a traditional distillery with tiny stills and worm tubs, you would expect a rather heavy whisky, but everything is done to lighten the spirit. The 12-year-old is a subtle dram with a fresh oak character. On the nose there is almost an scent of cricket bats or linseed oil which develops into a sweet leathery aroma with a drop of water. The sweetness on the tongue soon fades to a sharper, drier flavour and a lingering finish.

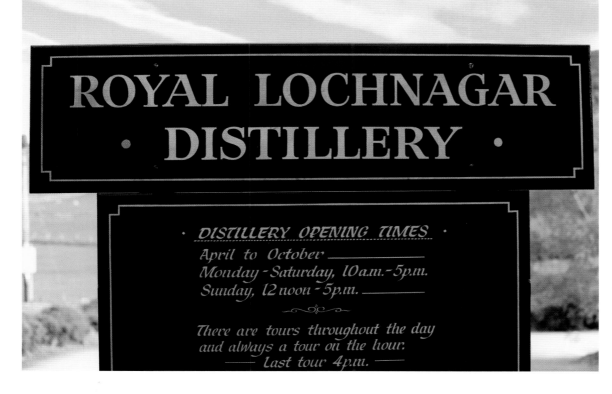

ABOVE When this cask was filled in 1986, the whisky loch was full to the brim and the distillery's future must have looked precarious to say the least.

LEFT The Royal Lochnagar Distillery has long been a popular tourist attraction in Royal Deeside.

CENTRAL HIGHLANDS AND THE WEST COAST

DISTILLING, LEGALLY OR OTHERWISE, WAS ONCE ENDEMIC RIGHT ACROSS THE HIGHLANDS FROM THE PERTHSHIRE GLENS TO THE WEST COAST. TODAY'S SURVIVORS AMONG THOSE OLD NINETEENTH CENTURY DISTILLERIES ARE FEW AND FAR BETWEEN AND, AS ISOLATED OUTPOSTS OF THE WHISKY INDUSTRY, THEY TEND TO HAVE LITTLE IN COMMON.

Most of the old Perthshire distilleries closed long ago. Those that survived tended to be tied to a blend like Bell's and its long association with *Blair Athol*. Licensed in the late 1790s, this farm distillery struggled to compete with all the local illicit stills, until resuscitated by Alexander Connacher in the 1820s. Within 60 years he was supplying malt to Arthur Bell & Sons in Perth, who finally bought the distillery in 1933, even though it remained mothballed until after the war. Blair Athol's moment of glory came in the 1970s when the company trebled production in a bid to make Bell's Britain's top-selling blend. The reward for this achievement was a hostile, and ultimately successful, takeover bid from Guinness PLC, which eventually evolved into Diageo.

Aberfeldy, by contrast, was tied to Dewar's White Label almost from the day it was established in 1898. According to family folklore it was near the croft from which the original John Dewar departed to walk to Perth, where he set up the family business in 1846. As well as an emotional bond there was sound commercial logic. Aberfeldy, on the banks of the Upper Tay, was connected by rail and had plentiful supplies of water. Having merged with arch-rival James Buchanan & Co. in 1915, the two firms became part of the Distillers Company. In 1998 Aberfeldy and its three sister distilleries were sold to Bacardi along with the Dewar's brand and Bombay Sapphire gin for an eye-popping £1.15 billion. Two years later Bacardi spent £2 million on turning Aberfeldy into the Dewar's World of Whisky, and while the distillery does produce a 12-year-old single malt, the focus is almost entirely on the Dewar's blend.

BANDIT COUNTRY

A similar approach has been taken by the much smaller *Glenturret* distillery near Crieff, which became home to "The Famous Grouse Experience"

ABOVE Created by Matthew Gloag & Sons of Perth, The Famous Grouse is now owned by the Edrington Group and claims to be Scotland's favourite dram.

LEFT Blair Athol; the spiritual home of Bells, which became the UK's top-selling Scotch whisky in the 1970s.

OPPOSITE Now well into its third century, Oban's distillery is almost as old as the town itself. Its survival is partly down to being chosen as the original West Coast whisky among Diageo's "Classic Malts".

in 2002. While Glenturret is the brand's spiritual home, its physical contribution to the blend in terms of malt whisky is small. To the south lies the last and most recent of the Perthshire distilleries, *Deanston*, housed in one of James Arkwright's late-eighteenth-century "satanic mills". The building only converted to whisky making in the 1960s.

Beyond Perthshire, on the way back towards Glasgow, is *Glengoyne*. Today as tourists flock northwards to the Trossachs, east of Loch Lomond, it is hard to believe this was once bandit country. It was full of cattle rustlers, like Sir Walter Scott's romantic hero Rob Roy, and whisky smugglers. Glengoyne was founded in 1833 by George Connell, right on the edge of the Highland line. Before long it was connected by rail to the big blending houses of Glasgow and Perth, and much of the malt began disappearing into Lang's Supreme, whose owners bought the distillery in the 1870s.

It was owned by the Lang Brothers for almost a century before coming into the fold of what became the Edrington Group. As its key blend declined, Glengoyne found itself overshadowed by its new stable-mates Macallan and Highland Park. Since 2003 it has thrived as part of the much smaller independent whisky company Ian Macleod Distillers.

WEST COAST

While the distilleries in the Central Highlands have been thinned out over the years, it is nothing to the cull on the West Coast. Since it was founded in 1794, out of what was originally a brewery, *Oban* has witnessed countless distilleries along the Argyll coast come and go. Today it appears small and rather quaint with its solitary pair of stills, and hemmed in by the town that has grown up around it. Oban was a tiny fishing village when brothers John and Hugh Stevenson established a boat-building yard, a tannery and finally a distillery. The Stevensons continued to make whisky for another two generations, though it was always a sideline to the family's other business interests.

Having passed out of family hands in the 1860s, Oban was acquired by a Mr J. Walter Higgin, who began slowly rebuilding the distillery in 1890, while continuing to make whisky there. By all accounts the malt was in strong demand from the blenders. Feeling constrained by lack of space, Higgin tried to burrow into the cliff behind the distillery to create a warehouse. In doing so he discovered a secret cave

and the bones of a Neolithic tribe – these now reside in the National Antiquities Museum in Edinburgh.

Apart from the rebuilding of the still-room in the 1960s, Oban has changed little since Higgin's day and has been in pretty much continual production except for six years during the 1930s. As part of the Distillers Company, now Diageo, it may have felt vulnerable at times as a far-flung supplier of malt whisky for blends, but its future was secured the day it joined the original line-up of Classic Malts in 1988.

It is over an hour's drive north beside Loch Linnhe to the other long-established West Coast distillery of *Ben Nevis*. It was founded in the shadow of Britain's tallest mountain by "Long John" Macdonald in 1825. By the 1880s such was the demand for "Long John's Dew of Ben Nevis" that a second Nevis distillery with seven stills had been built alongside, which was merged under one roof in 1908. Beside whisky, there was a sawmill and a farm with 200 head of cattle fed on the draff from the distillery. There was also a small fleet of steamers and a total workforce of 230.

A century later, with the farm and steamers long gone, the name "Long John" resurfaced as a popular blended Scotch owned by Whitbread, who acquired the distillery itself in 1981. A decade later Ben Nevis was sold to its current owners – the Japanese drinks giant, Nikka.

This West Coast single malt from Oban – the gateway to the Isles – has been a proud member of the Classic Malts since the start, yet the distillery's solitary pair of stills have struggled to keep up with demand. There is just not that much of it available in bottle. The limited releases often reserved for duty-free are often worth seeking out, but the one constant has been the 14-year-old. There is a brisk, fresh quality to this malt, immediately apparent on the nose. It is only moderately peated, but the smoke with its aromas of iodine and brine mingles with vanilla oak. On the tongue the malty flavours come through, adding a richer flavour and pleasing texture.

EDRADOUR
PITLOCHRY, PERTHSHIRE

WHEN THE BIG BOSSES OF THE WHISKY INDUSTRY WORRY ABOUT OVERPRODUCTION, AS THEY DO EVERY FEW DECADES OR SO, THE LAST PLACE THEY LOOK IS EDRADOUR IN THE HILLS BEYOND THE PERTHSHIRE TOWN OF PITLOCHRY. THIS DOLLS-HOUSE DISTILLERY IS ONE OF THE SMALLEST IN SCOTLAND, AND WITH AN ANNUAL PRODUCTION OF 90,000 GALLONS, IT PRODUCES WHAT A REASONABLY BIG MALT DISTILLERY MIGHT PUMP OUT IN A WEEK.

Edradour was built in 1837 by a group of local farmers, including Duncan Forbes who had been distilling legally in these parts since 1825 and no doubt illegally before then. Plenty of moonshine was being made in these remote, tucked away hills with their abundant access to water. Today Edradour is the sole survivor among seven farm distilleries in the small parish of Logierait, and now belongs to the independent bottler, Andrew Symington. One of the lost distilleries was Ballechin whose name lives on in a heavily peated expression of Edradour.

Symington was inspired to launch Ballechin after reading Alfred Barnard's account in his monumental guide to Britain's whisky distilleries written in the 1880s. Travelling through the parish by open carriage, he wrote of "the rich treasures of beauty spread out before us" and of the burns "which are associated at every secluded bend and shady corner with the smuggling bothy." Like many a Victorian convert to the new vice of whisky, Barnard was clearly entranced by the drink's illicit past, describing the smugglers as men of "remarkable muscular power and shrewd audacity".

Back in 1933, the distillery which then belonged to the Macintosh family, was bought as a barely going concern by W. Whitely & Co. for £1,050. William Whitely was one of the more colourful rogues in the trade who survived bankruptcy to launch the King's Ransom blend in 1928. It was soon claimed to be the most expensive whisky on the market, and its US

BELOW Edradour is a classic, small-scale farm distillery that has barely changed since Victorian times.

agent was none other than Mafia boss, Frank Costello. During Prohibition the brand along with its sister blend; The House of Lords, was smuggled into the States via the island of St Pierre, off the coast of Newfoundland.

Having made his own 'king's ransom' during Prohibition, Whitely passed the business to one of Costello's associates, Irving Haim who owned Edradour until he died in 1976. Six years later, the distillery was acquired by Pernod Ricard's then small whisky arm – Campbell Distillers who promptly opened it up to the public and in 1986 began bottling Edradour as a single malt, the first time its owners had ever done so. But the quantities produced were tiny and it never really fitted in with Pernod's growing portfolio of brands and distilleries. In 2002 it was sold to Symington who has preserved it as a thoroughly traditional distillery ever since.

Upstairs there was an old Morton's refrigerator that had been cooling the wort since the 1930s. When it finally packed in in 2009 most distillers would have replaced it with a modern heat exchanger, but not its new owners who insisted on an exact replica in stainless steel at considerable expense despite it having no tangible impact on the whisky. That one detail speaks volumes about Edradour's stubborn, some would say obsessive, belief in tradition.

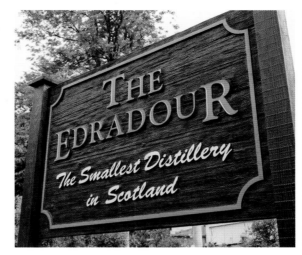

The rest of the process, from fermentation in Oregon pine wash-backs to distillation in two of the smallest stills legally operating in Scotland, happens in one downstairs room. Jostling for space with a quaint-looking spirits still, is an open topped mash tun that is as old as the distillery itself. As well as being almost comically small, the mash tun is brightly painted in red and green like an old carousel from a fairground. Until recently four men would clamber inside, once the mash was done, to shovel the residue out through a hole in the wall. Health and Safety put a stop to that.

WHISKY TASTING NOTES
EDRADOUR 10-YEAR-OLD DISTILLERY EDITION 40% ABV

The house style at Edradour could be described as relatively sweet and fruity, thanks to the way the spirit is distilled and the fondness for ex-sherry casks since Andrew Symington took over in 2002. A year later he began creating a separate, heavily peated line called Ballechin, which may show its best in ex-Bourbon wood. There is also a wide range of malts that have been finished or fully matured in wine casks such as Barolo, Burgundy, Madeira and Sauternes. The Distillery Edition 10-year-old offers hints of dried fruit and sherried sweetness on the nose and a trace of fruitcake and golden syrup on the tongue, before a mellow, oaky finish.

TOP It may be a dolls-house distillery, but there are undoubtedly smaller craft distillers than Edradour now operating since this sign was erected.

LEFT Edradour's pocket-sized mash tun is as old as the distillery itself.

GLENGOYNE
DUMGOYNE, NEAR KILLEARN, GLASGOW

THIS HANDSOME DISTILLERY LIES JUST ABOVE THE HIGHLAND LINE THAT CUTS SCOTLAND DIAGONALLY FROM THE NORTH EAST TO THE SOUTH WEST. IT LIES IN ROLLING FARMLAND JUST HALF AN HOUR'S DRIVE NORTH OF GLASGOW, YET AT THE TIME OF ITS BIRTH IN THE EARLY NINETEENTH CENTURY, THIS WAS A WILD AND REMOTE LAND OF BRIGANDS, CATTLE RUSTLERS AND ILLICIT STILLS.

Running down the steep, south-facing flank of Dumgoyne hill is a burn that cascades the last fifty feet into a pool, creating its own secret glen. Here, on the edge of the Highlands in the Campsie Fells, due north of Glasgow, is a perfect spot for an eighteenth-century bootlegger to set up his still. There was abundant, clear water for steeping the grain and condensing the spirity vapours into whisky, and there was seclusion from the powers that be. The area was popularized by Sir Walter Scott and his tales of Rob Roy a romantic outlaw in the mould of Robin Hood or Billy the Kid who once hid in a tree to escape capture 300 yards from Glengoyne distillery.

Among some thirteen illicit stills operating in the area was that of George Connell who was making moonshine on his Burnfoot farm, until he took out a license to distil in 1833. Over time his Burnfoot distillery became known as Glen Guin, Gaelic for the valley of the wild geese, and finally Glengoyne. It seems Connell instinctively knew the value of maturation since a warehouse that still stands was one of the first things he built at his new distillery. He also took out a 99-year lease on the land of Burnfoot of Glenguin for the princely sum of £8. Crucially the lease included "the privilege of taking the whole water of the said burn at any future time".

At first the whisky would have been sold to passing drovers bringing their cattle to market, but once the railway arrived in 1848 it began to flow south to Glasgow. At some point it caught the eye of Hugh Lang who ran a pub in the city's Broomielaw district on the banks of the Clyde. Initially he would have sold it as a "self whisky" - what we would now call a single malt, in five-gallon, stone jars straight from the cask. Before long he was using it to create his own blended whiskies, having established Lang Brothers Ltd with his three sons in 1861. From that point on, the fate of Glengoyne became increasingly tied to the success of the company's blends, notably Lang's Supreme.

In 1876 the Lang's decided it was time for a bit of vertical integration and bought the distillery. It remained in their hands as an independent family business right up until it was sold to the old Glasgow whisky firm of Robertson & Baxter in 1965. Within a year a second pair of stills had been installed to feed the growing demand for blended whisky after the war.

BELOW When a cask of Glengoyne fell off the back of a lorry in Glasgow, cups, tumblers and teapots appeared from nowhere while "housewives loaded with shopping walked away licking their fingers," reported the *Daily Record*.

At some point it was decided to release a Glengoyne single malt, but it was never a real focus as Robertson & Baxter evolved into the Edrington Group whose priority was always going to be Macallan, Famous Grouse and Highland Park. Overshadowed by its more famous siblings, Glengoyne remained somewhat lost, until it was rescued by Ian Macleod Distillers Ltd who bought the distillery in 2003 for £7.2 million.

As whisky blenders and brokers it was a big step for Ian Macleod to finally be distilling a whisky of its own, and for Glengoyne it was a much happier fit to be back in independent family hands. Yet Edrington did bequeath a fine inventory of sherry casks, and despite the rarity and expense of such barrels – costing at least five times more than their Bourbon equivalent – this wood policy has been continued by the new owners. The gentle new-make spirit which has never seen a whiff of peat smoke seems to be perfectly suited to sherry maturation.

Meanwhile the draff from the distillery is supplied to a local farmer to feed his herd of beef cattle, and the remaining residue is filtered through a new series of reed beds. It is all part of Glengoyne's plan to be as environmentally sustainable as possible.

ABOVE A decorative whisky barrel greets visitors to Glengoyne.

BELOW Glengoyne Distillery sits just over the Highland Line, while its warehouses across the road are in the Lowlands.

WHISKY TASTING NOTES
GLENGOYNE 10-YEAR-OLD 40% ABV

Using totally unpeated malt is pretty rare and lovers of Laphroaig may find this an underwhelming dram. Yet the absence of smoke means there's no place for Glengoyne or the distillery manager to hide. There's a naked purity to the spirit after a long fermentation and a very slow distillation, before it is filled into casks a third of which are a mixture of first-fill European and American oak sherry casks. Ten years later the whisky emerges with a slightly nutty, popcorn aroma with a grassy, green apple note that comes through on the palate. The texture turns oily with water.

SPEYSIDE

RISING IN THE MOUNTAINS SOUTH OF LOCH NESS, THE RIVER SPEY FLOWS NORTH-EAST FOR 100 MILES THROUGH BANFF AND MORAY TO THE SEA. THE VALLEY, KNOWN AS STRATHSPEY, MAY FEEL A LONG DRIVE FROM THE CENTRAL BELT, BUT THIS IS NOTHING COMPARED WITH HOW IT WAS BEFORE THE ADVENT OF MODERN ROADS AND RAILWAYS. THEN THIS CORNER OF SCOTLAND FELT FAR MORE REMOTE, AND THROUGH THE LONG WINTER MONTHS IT WOULD CLOSE IN ON ITSELF BEHIND THE VAST GRANITE BULK OF THE CAIRNGORMS. WHEN THE TRACKS AND UNPAVED ROADS WERE CLOGGED WITH SNOW, IT WOULD HAVE BEEN VIRTUALLY CUT OFF FROM THE OUTSIDE WORLD.

THE WHISKY HERITAGE OF SPEYSIDE

FOR THE BEST PART OF A CENTURY AFTER THE ACT OF UNION OF 1707, SPEYSIDE WAS, FOR THE GOVERNMENT, AN UNTAMED WILDERNESS. FOR THOSE LIVING HERE IT WAS OFTEN A CASE OF SUBSISTENCE FARMING. IN THE HIGHER GLENS OF SPEYSIDE, THERE WAS LITTLE POINT TRYING TO SELL THE MEAGRE CROP OF BARLEY IN THE MARKETS BY THE COAST, WHICH WERE SURROUNDED BY FERTILE FARMLAND. IF THERE WAS GRAIN TO SPARE, IT WAS BETTER TO DISTIL IT INTO WHISKY. THERE WAS CERTAINLY NO SHORTAGE OF CLEAR, FRESH WATER FOR WHISKY MAKING, AND PLENTY OF FUEL, IN THE SHAPE OF PEAT, TO MALT THE BARLEY AND FIRE THE STILLS.

As the authorities slowly stamped out illicit distillation through the Lowlands and Central Highlands, the whisky of this region became more valuable. By clamping down on Highland culture after the battle of Culloden in 1746, the authorities inadvertently turned whisky into a symbol of defiance. Meanwhile the big Lowland distillers had been encouraged to run their stills flat-out by the way they were taxed. What trickled off a small Highland pot still was bound to taste better even without the mellowing effect of slow maturation in wood.

There was one glen in Upper Speyside that seemed to specialize in illicit distillation. In the remote hills above the River Livet that flows into the Spey at Ballindalloch, there were countless stills in operation. So famous did Glenlivet whisky become, that King George IV asked for it by name when he set foot in Edinburgh on his famous state visit to Scotland in 1822. A modern equivalent would be Prince Charles asking for some Lebanese black on an official visit to Beirut. Word reached Elizabeth Grant of Rothiemurchus, near Aviemore, that the

BELOW Thomas Telford's famous cast-iron bridge over the Spey at Craigellachie, built between 1812 and 1814, is still carrying pedestrians and cyclists. It was the advent of decent roads and railways that really opened up Speyside as a whisky region.

Lord Chamberlain "was looking everywhere for pure Glenlivet whisky". She wrote later of how she went to empty her "petbin where the whisky was long in wood, long in uncorked bottles, mild as milk and with the true contraband goût in it".

Within a few years the region's distillers began to drift in from the cold and take out licences. The distilleries remained small and often seasonal affairs – an adjunct to the main business of farming. It was not until the great boom in blended whisky towards the end of the nineteenth century that Speyside took off as a whisky region. The advent of the railways was far more important to the development of Speyside as the greatest source of malt whisky in Scotland, and yet those early tales of illicit distillation up in Glen Livet played a crucial role. Victorians loved the romance of the noble savage distilling in his cave surrounded by towering mountains and rutting stags. Landseer's famous painting of the illicit still went straight to their sentimental heart, and was a theme often revisited by the early pioneers of whisky marketing.

BELOW Architectural plans for Benromach distillery drawn up by Charles Doig in 1896. Note the pagoda roof that came to symbolise all the late Victorian distilleries designed by Doig.

ABOVE Before Speyside there was Glenlivet, the most famous distillery in the whole of Scotland in its day.

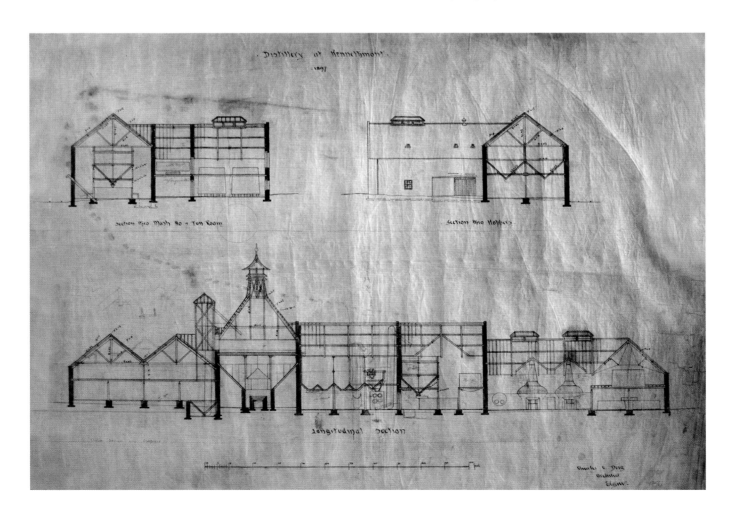

GLENLIVET WITH EVERYTHING

Leaving aside the long-forgotten Ferrintosh distillery near Dingawall on the Black Isle, Glenlivet was the first real brand of malt whisky in Scotland, though originally the name referred to the glen itself, rather than the distillery. When the first blenders came here in search of malt for their blends they did not ask for Speyside whisky but rather Glenlivet, or at least whisky made in the same style. It was perhaps just as well the other distillers jumped on the bandwagon and hyphenated their names to add Glenlivet, since the actual distillery of that name founded by George Smith in 1824 would never have coped with demand.

In 1867 the Strathspey railway line opened, and its stations of Ballindalloch, Aberlour, Craigellachie and Knockando became synonymous with whisky. Distillers flocked to follow John Smith's example at Cragganmore, and set up their stills beside the tracks with a siding to speed up the ebb and flow of grain and whisky. All the barley was malted at the distilleries, but increasingly coal and coke were used to fire the kilns. Less peat smoke created a lighter, less tarry malt which appealed to the blenders and may largely explain why Speyside became a favoured source of whisky among the late-nineteenth-century blenders.

Between 1886 and 1899 no fewer than 23 distilleries were built on Speyside, in what was the most dramatic building boom the whisky industry has ever seen.

If people spoke of a speculative bubble waiting to burst, they were right. The early decades of the twentieth century were extremely tough, with the First World War, US Prohibition and the Great Depression. Many Speyside distilleries spent years in mothballs waiting for an upturn in blended Scotch. Distillers went bust, merged or were bought out, often by the ever-growing Distillers Company, now Diageo. Today there are over 40 distilleries on Speyside, way more than in any other whisky region, and, as of 2015, most are working flat-out to supply's the world's newfound thirst for Scotch.

While the modern age of single-malt whisky started here with Glenfiddich in the 1960s, the term "Speyside" does not pack the same punch as "Islay". Successful malts like Macallan and Glenlivet rely on the power of their brand, rather than their provenance. For many of the others, it is hard to stand out on Speyside as a single malt. It is even difficult to describe the style of the region, except with vague references to a heathery sweetness and little, if any, use of peat.

BELOW An etching from the 1890s showing a giant pair of worm tubs at Glenlivet – a name that defined this whisky region well before it became known as Speyside. A good number of distilleries, some way downstream, bolted the "G" word to their own, in the hope of some reflected glory.

ABOVE Macallan, which once clung to the tag-line "–Glenlivet", now stands firmly on its own two feet, a little aloof perhaps, but confident of being one of the finest malts in Speyside.

LEFT Checking how much whisky remained in the casks at Knockando (circa 1972) and how much had been siphoned off by those pesky Angels.

GLENFIDDICH
DUFFTOWN, BANFFSHIRE

AS A DISTILLERY, GLENFIDDICH IS WELL INTO ITS THIRD CENTURY, HAVING BEEN FOUNDED IN 1887; AS THE MOST POPULAR SINGLE MALT ON THE PLANET, HOWEVER, GLENFIDDICH IS A CHILD OF THE 1960S. THEN AGAIN, SINGLE MALTS BARELY EXISTED BEFORE THIS INDEPENDENT SPEYSIDE DISTILLERY TAUGHT THE WORLD THERE WAS MORE TO WHISKY THAN BLENDED SCOTCH. IT WAS IN 1963 THAT IT LAUNCHED ITSELF IN ITS TRADEMARKED TRIANGULAR DARK GREEN BOTTLE.

The rest of the industry was faintly bemused, given the widespread belief that malt whisky was too robust a flavour to ever catch on beyond a tiny handful of drinkers. According to received wisdom, distillers existed for one reason only. Their job was to provide the base ingredients for blenders to turn into a smooth, consistent spirit to satisfy whisky drinkers from Seoul to San Francisco. Fifty years on, Glenfiddich has more than disproved that idea, and today you can drink the single malt made by virtually every malt distillery in Scotland whether bottled by the owners or by a third party.

All this was way into the future when William Grant took the plunge to start his own business and leave his job as a bookkeeper at Mortlach, the first distillery in Dufftown. When his original plan to open a lime works came to nothing in 1871, he returned to Mortlach,

where another idea slowly began to take shape. He would build a distillery of his own, but it took 16 years to acquire the confidence and the necessary funds to do so. With a wife and nine children to support on an annual salary of £100, plus £7 as precentor at the Free Church of Dufftown, it was never going to be an overnight decision.

Glenfiddich was cobbled together from second-hand stills and equipment bought from Elizabeth Cumming, the lady distiller at what is now Cardhu. The distillery itself cost £650 and used stones dug from the bed of the River Fiddich, a nearby tributary of the Spey. The water to steep the barley and help make the spirit came from the Robbie Dhu spring, while a small burn provided the power for a malt mill.

The distillery somehow survived the great whisky crash at the start of the twentieth century, as well as

LEFT Just two of the two dozen Oregon pine washbacks where the wort is fermented into the wash at the distillery that pioneered the modern era of single malt whisky in the 1960s.

OPPOSITE NEAR ABOVE Glenfiddich claims that it is the only Highland whisky to be bottled at source and use the same water throughout the process.

OPPOSITE NEAR BELOW Some of the older expressions including the Glenfiddich 50-year-old, available from the distillery shop for £22,000 (as of 2015).

OPPOSITE FAR RIGHT In 1969 Glenfiddich built a visitors' centre and threw open its doors to the public. At first the whisky industry was sceptical the idea would catch on, but more than half Scotland's distilleries have since followed suit.

the First World War and Prohibition in the USA. By the time William Grant died in 1923, much of the malt was being used in the company's own blends. The odd bottle even reached as far as Vancouver in one direction and Adelaide in the other. The self-sufficient, defiantly independent nature of William Grant & Sons survives to this day.

THE GLENFIDDICH TRIANGLE

In the post-war years, the company had to compete against a rather overbearing Distillers Company who threatened to choke off supplies of grain whisky unless Grant's stopped supplying the big brewers with blended Scotch. Having installed its own coppersmiths and cooperage in the late 1950s, the firm built its own grain distillery at Girvan in 1963. By then the distillery was producing a 5-year-old whisky called Glenfiddich Pure Malt – a niche brand sold only in Scotland. This was replaced with an 8-year-old which was made available south of the border. From there it spread to duty-free and eventually the world beyond.

Glenfiddich's triangular bottle helped it stand out, and businessmen claimed to like the way it fitted into their slim, Samsonite briefcases. Others appreciated how it stacked easily in a cellar, while one woman, possibly with tongue in cheek, praised the way it didn't roll out of bed like other bottles. At first the sales team found it difficult to persuade hotels and bars to stock a single malt, since no one had ever asked for one. Yet in

terms of price and packaging it was really sold as an alternative to deluxe blends like Chivas Regal and Johnnie Walker Black Label. Because these were 12-year-old whiskies, Glenfiddich soon found it had to raise its age accordingly.

Those marketing Glenfiddich in the early days were certainly inventive. Seeing that actors invariably drank cold tea instead of Scotch when having a dram on stage, it was decided to bottle a line of the whisky with flat ginger ale. It certainly beat yesterday's PG Tips, and soon bottles began to appear in London's West End, giving the brand some much-needed free publicity.

In 1969, Glenfiddich pioneered the idea of whisky tourism by throwing open its doors to the public for free, and encouraging them to spend money in the visitors' centre and distillery shop. Again the Scotch whisky establishment was sceptical that anyone would want to look round a factory, yet before long there were plenty of similar distillery visitor centres.

With its cooperage, copper-smithy and bottling hall surrounded by endless warehouses, Glenfiddich is a hive of industry. Its 29 stills pump out sufficient spirit for a current annual production of 1.1 million cases of single malt spread over a core range of age-statements, including 12, 15, 18 and 21-year-old, and a raft of special editions. Among the rarest expressions have been the 55-year-old Janet Sheed Roberts Reserve. She was William Grant's last surviving granddaughter – and Scotland's oldest woman when she died in 2012 aged 110.

WHISKY TASTING NOTES
GLENFIDDICH 15-YEAR-OLD SOLERA RESERVE 40% ABV

The name Glenfiddich may be slightly tarnished for malt whisky aficionados, if only because of the tall poppy syndrome – the main expression is ubiquitous and the distillery itself is huge. But there is a lot more to Glenfiddich than its light, grassy 12-year-old that gave so many whisky drinkers their first taste of single malts.

The main ingredient is 15-year-old whisky from ex-bourbon barrels, but some is aged in virgin oak and some in sherry casks. All three are then tipped into a Solera vat, the sort you might find in Jerez, and married together. The result is an orange-scented, lightly sherried whisky with some sweet spice, raisins and fruitcake.

GLENLIVET
BALLINDALLOCH, BANFFSHIRE

"THE SINGLE MALT THAT STARTED IT ALL" IS HOW GLENLIVET SEES ITSELF. THE GLEN IN QUESTION IN UPPER SPEYSIDE WAS FAMOUS FOR ITS ILLICIT STILLS. ACCORDING TO ONE LOCAL FARMER, "THERE WERE NOT THREE PERSONS IN GLENLIVET IN THOSE DAYS [IN THE EARLY 1800S] WHO WERE NOT ENGAGED DIRECTLY OR INDIRECTLY IN THE TRADE." IN LATE AUTUMN AFTER THE HARVEST, WHEN THE SMUGGLING BOTHIES WERE MOST ACTIVE, THE SWEET SCENT OF DISTILLED SPIRIT MUST HAVE FILLED THE AIR. THE GLEN CAME TO DEFINE A STYLE OF WHISKY WELL BEFORE ANYONE SPOKE OF SPEYSIDE AS A WHISKY REGION. INDEED SO FAMOUS WAS THE WORD "GLENLIVET" THAT A TRAIL OF DISTILLERIES ALMOST TO THE COAST BOLTED ITS NAME ON TO THEIRS IN THE HOPE OF SOME REFLECTED GLORY.

The Glenlivet distillery ought to have been flattered, though in truth its rivals were really using the glen with a small "g" as a generic type. It wasn't that they wanted to be mistaken for the whisky-making venture of George Smith who became the first licensed distiller in these parts. In 1822, when every drop of whisky in the glen was moonshine, no less a figure than King George IV was asking for some Glenlivet when he arrived in Edinburgh on his famous state visit. It was the first time a British monarch had set foot north of the border since 1650 and the whole event was stage managed by Walter Scott. Swathed in tartan, with his gouty legs wrapped in pink tights, "the portly Hanoverian" might seem almost comic, as though auditioning for a part in a forerunner to *Brigadoon*. Yet the Scottish establishment took him very seriously indeed, and began to embrace the romanticism of the Highlands.

A WARM WELCOME

Two years later, in 1824, George Smith obtained a licence to make whisky at his farm of Upper Drummin which had been leased from the Duke of Gordon by his father. Within three years the new venture was on the brink of bankruptcy and Smith had to go cap in hand to the Duke's factor. In return for abandoning the lease on a neighbouring farm and selling off his cattle he received

BELOW LEFT George Smith, the first man to take out a distiller's licence in the parish of Glenlivet in 1824. Having struggled at first with hostile neighbours and near bankruptcy, he eventually became one of the most successful and recognized distillers in Scotland.

BELOW Compared to Glenfiddich, Glenlivet was slow to join the single malt revolution, but it has been making up for lost time. It has long been the most popular malt in America and may one day overtake its arch-rival.

a £500 rescue package. At the time he was being routinely intimidated by all the illicit distillers in the glen, who didn't take kindly to the new Glenlivet distillery. As Smith wrote of his venture: "I was warned before I began by my civil neighbours that they meant to burn my new distillery to the ground, and me in the heart of it." Not surprisingly he made sure he always carried a pair of hair-trigger pistols that he had been given by a local laird.

By 1830 most of the smugglers and moonshine operators had either been flushed out of the region or had been encouraged to take out a licence. Before long, Smith was selling his Glenlivet malt to blenders in Aberdeen, Perth and the Port of Leith. Among his customers was Andrew Usher, the man dubbed "the father of blended Scotch". In 1853, Usher launched his pioneering "Old Vatted Glenlivet". Today it would be designated a blended malt, since it did not contain grain whisky like Usher's Green Stripe and the plethora of blends that followed.

The distillery moved down the glen to its current home to be nearer to the newly opened Strathspey railway line. Production jumped to 4,000 gallons a week and the casks were taken by horse and cart to Ballindalloch station. Smith became a minor celebrity among distillers, with newspapers keen to know about him, and by the time he died in 1871, Glenlivet was clearly the best-known distillery in Scotland. It was said

that over 100 casks a year were being sold in London, though it is unclear whether the malt was blended up by publicans and grocers or served in its original form. In 1882 George Smith's heirs managed to reduce the number of distillers piggy-backing on their name to just 10 after a costly two-year tussle in the courts.

Glenlivet would have been the obvious contender to lead the great malt whisky renaissance in the 1960s. Indeed it could have done so 80 years earlier, being the only vaguely recognizable brand among single malts. Instead it was left to Glenfiddich, while Glenlivet spent the sixties selling most of its malt to blenders, in common with Glen Grant and Longmorn, with which it had merged as a limited company. The one exception was the USA, where Glenlivet has long been the bestselling single malt. It was a market first developed by Bill Smith Grant after Prohibition, when the distillery started to bottle some of its own whisky instead of selling it all in cask.

In 1977 Glenlivet and its sister distilleries were bought by Seagram's, whose key focus was the Chivas Regal blend. Then, in 2001 Seagram's spirits division was carved up, with most of the whisky going to the French group, Pernod Ricard. Its single malt sales climbed to over 600,000, pushing Glenlivet up to second position behind Glenfiddich. In 2010 a £10 million expansion was announced, adding six stills to the existing 14 and boosting the overall capacity by 75 per cent. Glenfiddich's days in pole position may be numbered.

WHISKY TASTING NOTES
THE GLENLIVET XXV, 43% ABV

This gold-medal-winning whisky is one of the super premium whiskies produced by George and JG Smith. After 25 years' maturation in cask, the final couple of years are spent in specially selected ex-Oloroso sherry butts, which adds an extra dimension of dried fruit, orange, dark chocolate and a crème brûlée sweetness to the floral, honey and candied fruit found on the original spirit. This is a rich and opulent dram with a warming cinnamon spice note and very definite hints of Christmas cake with its dried fruit and nutty elements. The finish is long and satisfying with ginger and a creamy orange edge to the balanced finish. A warm and satisfying whisky for a cold winter's evening.

ABOVE The name Glenlivet was widely used by whisky blenders like Watson's of Dundee. Initially it would have been a blend of malts until it included grain whisky. How much actually came from the Glenlivet distillery as opposed to the region in general is unclear.

LEFT Having moved his distillery down the glen, from its original site at Upper Drummin, George Smith sent his whisky by cart to be loaded on to trains on the Strathspey line. Before long Glenlivet was producing up to 4,000 gallons a week.

THE MACALLAN
CRAIGELLACHIE, BANFFSHIRE

IN JANUARY 2014 A SIX-LITRE LALIQUE DECANTER OF MACALLAN M, ONE OF ONLY FOUR PRODUCED, BECAME THE MOST EXPENSIVE WHISKY EVER SOLD AT AUCTION. THE WHISKY HAD BEEN SELECTED FROM SEVEN SHERRY CASKS, THE OLDEST DATING FROM 1940, AND THE FINAL PRICE WHEN KNOCKED DOWN BY SOTHEBY'S IN HONG KONG WAS A JAW-DROPPING US$628,205. TWO YEARS EARLIER A BOTTLE OF THE MACALLAN 50-YEAR-OLD APPEARED IN THE JAMES BOND MOVIE *SKYFALL*. IT WAS NO MERE PRODUCT PLACEMENT, LIKE THE BOTTLE OF HEINEKEN WHICH FEATURES FOR A BRIEF MOMENT EARLIER IN THE FILM. IN ITS SCENE MACALLAN PLAYS AN ALMOST STARRING ROLE.

It has been quite a journey for what began as a humble farm distillery that first obtained a licence in 1824. Its founder was Alexander Reid, a tenant farmer who took out a lease on Easter Elchies farm on the west bank of the River Spey, a mile from Craigellachie. Reid had doubtless been selling moonshine to the drovers who would pass by on their journey to the big cattle markets of the Central Belt. They would pause for a while, buy a little whisky and then cross the river at a nearby ford.

It was originally known as the Elchies distillery, and by 1880 production had climbed to around 40,000 gallons a year. By then it belonged to James Stewart, a grain merchant who teamed up with three local bankers, including William Grant and Robert Dick, to raise funds. He planned to expand Macallan and build a second distillery – Glenrothes in the nearby town of Rothes – but it seems he became overstretched.

In 1892 Macallan was bought by Rodney Kemp, a self-made man with plenty of experience in the drinks trade, having been a wine merchant in Elgin and a partner in the Talisker distillery on Skye. Six years later William Grant and Robert Dick had become founders of Highland Distillers, and now they made an unsolicited bid to buy Macallan. Kemp was unimpressed with their offer of £80,000 and it was not until almost a century later that Highland Distillers finally managed to acquire Macallan in 1996. By then the price of the distillery had risen to £180 million.

Kemp disposed of his wine business to concentrate on the distillery, restoring the buildings, improving the equipment and boosting production to 2,500 gallons a week. By the time of his death in 1909, Macallan's whisky was well regarded by the blenders, but as a single malt it was all but unknown.

RIGHT Macallan has cleverly maintained its premium, well-crafted image, despite the burgeoning scale of production. By 2014 it boasted 21 stills, and has since announced a £100 million expansion plan.

The distillery remained in family hands for most of the twentieth century, initially through Kemp's sons-in-law, first Alexander Harbison and then Samuel Shiach, who took charge in 1938.

Throughout this time the distillery had barely changed since the end of the nineteenth century, except for an additional pair of bonded warehouses. A little Macallan seeped into the States during Prohibition, but the home market shrank by a third. Somehow production kept going apart from the 1932–33 season during the Depression and for a year during the Second World War. Gordon Shiach, an intelligence officer who had interrogated Hermann Goering at the Nuremberg trials, took over the distillery in 1947, but was killed in a road accident the following year.

DON'T LOOK NOW

In the 1950s the distillery was rebuilt with a new, glass-plated still-house and there was a steady expansion of warehouses with one built every year. By 1970 production had hit one million gallons, by which point some casks were being set aside for a single malt. In 1978 the first bottles of Macallan 10-year-old were released, though not too many people heard about it. The firm had only started advertising in 1974 with an annual budget of £25, though a bottle of Macallan did appear in Nicolas Roeg's classic film *Don't Look Now* released the year before.

Its screen appearance on a bedside table in a Venice hotel room was fair enough given the scriptwriter was Allan Schiach, who combined his role as chairman of Macallan-Glenlivet with writing screenplays. Yet it is doubtful many in the audience noticed the whisky, given what was happening on the bed between Julie Christie and Donald Sutherland.

Macallan's use of Glenlivet in its title was common practice among Speyside distilleries, but this was quietly dropped as the distillery built its reputation for its single malt. Being relatively quick off the mark in the burgeoning malt whisky market, gave it a head start. Today it rivals Glenlivet for second place behind Glenfiddich in terms of sales of single malts.

One of the great cornerstones of Macallan's quality, part of its DNA, was the insistence on sherry casks to mature the spirit. Yet clearly bourbon casks were being used for some time as well, to allow the distillery to launch its Fine Oak range in 2004. More recently Macallan's owners, the Edrington Group, took the radical step of dropping age-statements for its new 1824 series which starts with "Gold" and "Amber" and rises in price to "Sienna" and "Ruby". Macallan has always insisted the colour of its whiskies is entirely natural, with no spirit caramel added.

Dropping age-statements was at least partly to cope with demand for its aged whiskies. For years production has been trying to catch up. In 2008 it expanded the number of its "famously small stills" to 21 at a cost of £20 million. Then, in 2014, it announced plans for a further £100 million expansion, due for completion by 2017.

WHISKY TASTING NOTES
THE MACALLAN SIENNA 43% ABV

Rather than use age-statements to differentiate its various expressions, Macallan has taken a bold and somewhat controversial decision to use colour, although in some markets like the US you can still find the classic 12-year-old. Because the whiskies are natural shades with no spirit caramel added, the colour reflects the condition of the cask – how active it is, and how long the spirit spent in it. Sienna sits above "Gold" and "Amber", but below "Ruby".

As the colour suggests, there is a real dried fruit richness which is there on the nose along with cloves, ginger and candied orange peel. On the tongue the fruit becomes obvious, with notes of figs and Christmas pudding as well.

LEFT A traditional dunnage warehouse showing some 500-litre sherry butts in the foreground. Sherry wood was once insisted on for all Macallan's malts, but that rule has been quietly dropped to allow bourbon barrels as well.

CRAGGANMORE
BALLINDALLOCH, BANFFSHIRE

JOHN SMITH, WHO FOUNDED THE CRAGGANMORE DISTILLERY IN 1869, WAS SAID TO BE THE ILLEGITIMATE SON OF GEORGE SMITH OF GLENLIVET. WHETHER THAT WAS TRUE OR NOT, THE MAN HAD SPEYSIDE WHISKY IN HIS BLOOD BY THE TIME HE EMBARKED ON HIS OWN DISTILLERY, HAVING BEEN MANAGER OF GLENLIVET AND MACALLAN FOLLOWED BY A SPELL AS THE LEASEHOLDER AT GLENFARCLAS BEFORE THE GRANT FAMILY TOOK OVER IN 1865.

Around this time Smith persuaded his landlord, Sir George Macpherson-Grant, to lease him a plot of land at Ballindalloch where he founded Cragganmore, which means "great rock" in Gaelic. It was close to the newly opened Strathspey railway line that ran from Dufftown to Abernethy where it connected with the Great North of Scotland Railway. John Smith was a true railway buff and quickly built a siding connecting his new distillery to the track so grain could flow in and whisky could flow out.

The venture prospered, and before long Smith had moved into a smart Scots-baronial house complete with a turret and crenulations. He loved travelling by train, but had to do so in the guard's van, since he could not squeeze his 22-stone bulk in through the carriage doors, even sideways. By the time of his premature death in 1886, the so-called whisky express, carrying up to 16,000 gallons of Scotch whisky in cask, was a regular feature rattling along the Strathspey line.

KEEPING IT IN THE FAMILY

Cragganmore was producing 90,000 gallons a year when Gordon Smith inherited the distillery from his father. Most of its whisky was sent south to the Dundee blending firm of James Watson & Co. that eventually became part of the Dewar's empire.

BELOW Cragganmore had always been in demand from blenders as one of the more complex Speyside whiskies around, and there was no surprise when it was picked to represent the region in the original line-up of the six "Classic Malts".

By 1901, having barely missed a fortnight's production since inception, Smith decided the distillery needed rebuilding and hired Charles Doig – the leading distillery architect of his day. His design with the compact, whitewashed courtyard is what you see today.

UNIQUE STILLS

The two wash stills which feed the pair of spirit stills are unique in the industry. They appear to have been sawn off at the neck, with their lyne arm, which carries the vapours to the worm tubs, jutting out like a branch. No one knows whether they were specially designed to fit the original space, but they clearly work.

New-make Cragganmore has a robust, almost Highland character which matures into one of the more complex Speyside malts. It was always well regarded by the blenders, and in 1988 was picked to represent Speyside in the original line-up of the "Classic Malts".

WHISKY TASTING NOTES
CRAGGANMORE 12-YEAR-OLD 40% ABV

When it was decided to launch the Classic Malts to represent the whisky regions, Diageo's predecessor was spoilt for choice when it came to Speyside. The choice of Cragganmore was a good one and the 12-year-old has stood the test of time. It has the floral elegance of a Speyside, but a real depth and complexity too.

The nose manages to combine the fresh scent of cut grass and herbs with honey, nuts and baked fruit, as well as some sweetness from the American oak. On the tongue it has a soft, rounded texture and some ripe fruit from the malt, and you might pick up a very faint wisp of smoke on the finish.

BELOW The Cragganmore 12 year-old has the floral elegance of a classic Speyside, albeit with more depth and complexity.

ABOVE The wrought iron entrance to this much admired Speyside distillery of Cragganmore.

GLENROTHES
ROTHES, BANFFSHIRE

EVERY YEAR THE SPEYSIDE TOWN OF ROTHES PRODUCES THE EQUIVALENT OF FIFTY MILLION BOTTLES OF SINGLE MALT, THOUGH OF COURSE THE VAST MAJORITY OF IT DISAPPEARS INTO BLENDS, WHICH IS ONE REASON WHY THE TOWN APPEARS COY ABOUT ITS MAIN INDUSTRY. OF ITS FOUR DISTILLERIES, THE MOST HIDDEN – TUCKED DOWN A LEAFY GORGE BESIDE THE ROTHES BURN – IS GLENROTHES.

Its founder, James Stuart, was looking to build something bigger and better than Macallan, the small farm distillery he had owned since 1868. He found what he was looking for in a disused sawmill with a nearby spring to supply water, and the burn to supply power via a waterwheel. Work began in 1878, the year Britain was plunged into the worst financial crash for almost a century. His partners, Robert Dick and Willie Grant, worked for the Caledonian bank and had borrowed heavily from it. With the bank on the verge of collapse, they suddenly found themselves in charge of Glenrothes as Stuart decided to return to Macallan.

The new venture only survived with financial help from a local farmer, a retired rear admiral and the Presbyterian minister from nearby Archiestown who lent the distillery £600. Within five years Glenrothes was turning a profit supplying the Glasgow-based brokers and blenders – Robertson & Baxter. In 1887 it was decided to merge with Bunnahabhain on Islay and form the Highland Distillers company. For over a century, until it acquired Macallan in 1996, Glenrothes, or "The Heilan" as it was affectionately known, was the jewel in the company's crown. Since then Highland Distillers has become part of the Edrington Group.

In 1900, Glenrothes was producing 300,000 gallons from its four stills, and remained in almost continuous production until 1933 despite a dramatic fire the previous decade which sent a torrent of

BELOW As a key filling for popular blends like Cutty Sark and Famous Grouse, it seemed there was never any Glenrothes to spare to lay down casks for a single malt. That finally changed in 1994 with the release of the first Vintage Malt.

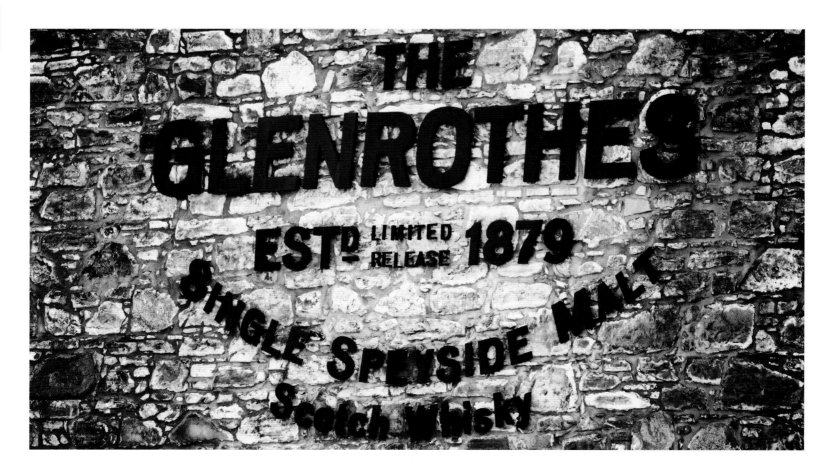

flaming whisky into the Rothes burn. People flocked to scoop up the escaping nectar, and the trout had never been so easy to catch, according to the local paper.

As a key component in Cutty Sark and other brands like Famous Grouse, almost every drop of Glenrothes was swallowed up by the blenders until 1994 when a limited amount was released as a vintage malt through Berry Brothers & Rudd in London. This venerable wine and spirit merchant owed its fortune to Cutty Sark – the blend it created in 1923. In recent years Berry Bros. has taken control of the Glenrothes single malt in return for giving the Edrington Group Cutty Sark.

WHISKY TASTING NOTES
GLENROTHES 2001 43% ABV

Joining the single malt revolution a little later than most, Glenrothes decided on a different tack. Rather than produce standard age-statement whiskies like a 10- or 15-year-old, Glenrothes chose to select casks from a particular year when the spirit had reached full maturity and release it as a vintage. The 2001 is an interesting play on wood, probably mainly ex-bourbon barrels with some sherry butts as well, though the recipe remains secret. On the nose there is lemon sherbet, some honey, some freshly cut wood and some baked fruit from the malt. The taste has a zesty citrus character with vanilla ice-cream and a hint of that raisin sweetness you find in PX sherry. In a word it's beguiling, exotic and hard to resist.

LEFT In keeping with this generous spirit, miniatures of Glenrothes come double sized.

BELOW Glenrothes by night when all you can hear is the muted thrum of machiney and the babbling of the Rothes burn.

GLEN GRANT
ROTHES, BANFFSHIRE

ONE OF GLEN GRANT'S CLAIMS TO FAME IS THAT THIS DISTILLERY IS UNIQUE IN BEING NAMED AFTER ITS FOUNDING FAMILY. JOHN AND JAMES GRANT HAD BEEN PARTNERS IN THE ABERLOUR DISTILLERY WHEN THEY FOUNDED GLEN GRANT IN ROTHES IN 1840. JOHN GRANT WAS A DISTILLER, WHILE HIS BROTHER WAS AN ENGINEER AND LOCAL POLITICIAN.

Within a year of opening their new venture the Grants began lobbying for the Elgin to Craigellachie railway to be extended via Rothes. In the end they helped bankroll the new line with a £4,500 cheque in 1858. For years Glen Grant remained the only distillery in Rothes and in 1872 passed to John Grant's nephew, James Grant, who was universally known as "the Major". When not driving around in the Highlands' first registered motorcar like a Scottish "Mr Toad", he could be found flogging the Spey with his fly rod or big-game hunting in Africa. He returned from one safari in what is now Zimbabwe with a young boy he had found abandoned by the roadside. It seems the boy, who was rechristened Biawa, had been orphaned after a tribal feud and "the Major" decided he would be better off

in Rothes. He went to the local school, became a lifelong supporter of Rothes FC and allegedly even played for them in goal occasionally.

Back in 1898, such was the success of Glen Grant that it was decided to build another distillery across the road with copies of the original stills. The prosaically named Glen Grant No.2 boasted a whisky pipe above the traffic that connected it to its mother distillery like an umbilical cord. The pipe was something Customs & Excise insisted upon, but it ran dry four years later. The new distillery did not reopen until 1965, when it was rechristened Caperdonich. It closed in 2002 and was finally demolished in 2010. The Major died in 1931, having outlived all but one of his eight children. His grandson Douglas Mackessack took over and became

BELOW In 1961 Armando Giovinetti, began importing casks of Glen Grant to Italy for bottling as a single malt. Within 20 years it had become the country's biggest-selling whisky.

one of the last "gentleman distillers" in Speyside. In 1977 he bowed to commercial pressure and sold Glen Grant to Seagram, who had long been using its malt in Chivas Regal. The new owners set about restoring the distillery's famous gardens, where Major Grant used to take gue sts for a moonlit tour after dinner. They would pass conservatories full of orchids and exotic fruits, walk across lawns bordered by rhododendrons and majestic copper beach trees and continue up a path beside a burn. The party would stop by a gorge where the Major would unlock a small safe embedded in the rock to produce glasses and a bottle of Glen Grant. While the conservatories have gone, the gardens and the whisky safe remain.

WHISKY TASTING NOTES
GLEN GRANT 10-YEAR-OLD 40% ABV

The single malt from this Speyside distillery was always best known in Italy. For years its very gentle, straw-coloured 5-year-old was the country's most popular Scotch whisky of all, and you would find bottles of it behind virtually every bar. Since 2005 Glen Grant has been owned by Campari, the Italian spirits giant. Older, rarer expressions have long been available from independent bottlers such as Gordon & MacPhail. The standard 10-year-old bottled by Campari acts as a delicate, grassy, toffee-scented introduction to Speyside. It may not be the most complex single malt but it is balanced and well made with a soft, baked apple and cut grass flavour and a relatively short finish.

LEFT Glen Grant boasts the best landscaped gardens of any distillery, and a walk along the burn where Major Grant kept his whisky safe is a must.

BELOW Sporting the best mutton-chop whiskers on Speyside, John Grant (LEFT) was succeeded by his nephew (RIGHT). Major James Grant was the classic Victorian gentleman distiller with a penchant for big-game hunting in Africa and salmon fishing on the Spey.

CARDHU
ARCHIESTOWN, BANFFSHIRE

JOHN CUMMING HAD BEEN BUSTED FOR SMUGGLING WHISKY MANY TIMES AND HAD A STRING OF CONVICTIONS TO PROVE IT. IT WAS PROBABLY HIS WIFE, HELEN, WHO ACTUALLY MADE THE WHISKY AT CARDOW FARM, WHICH HE LEASED IN 1811. THERE WERE FOLK TALES OF HOW SHE WOULD TREAT THE EXCISEMEN TO TEA IN HER KITCHEN WHILE HER HUSBAND HOISTED A RED FLAG IN THE YARD TO WARN ANYONE NEARBY WITH AN ILLICIT STILL.

In 1824 Cumming took out a licence, and though it remained a small-scale farm distillery at least the whisky could now be transported openly rather than be smuggled over the hills. On his death in 1846 the distillery passed to his daughter Elizabeth and her husband. When widowed in 1872, she became the first lady distiller on Speyside. Fifteen years later she sold the original stills to William Grant for his new venture at Glenfiddich, and drew up plans for a new distillery. According to the whisky writer Alfred Barnard, the buildings were "of the most straggling and primitive description and although water power existed, a great part of the work was done by manual labour". Cardow was rebuilt in 1893 and then sold to John Walker & Sons on condition the family would

continue running it. Most of the production was sent for blending, though there were early adverts for Cardow as "a single whisky". Elizabeth's son John Cumming took over, and by the 1920s had ensured that all the distillery workers' cottages had running water, electric light and even indoor toilets. Meanwhile the distillery continued to supply Johnnie Walker and other blends of the Distillers Company, whose chairman was later Sir Ronald Cumming, Elizabeth's grandson.

After a pause in distilling during the Second World War, production was cranked up to meet the surging demand for Johnnie Walker. The distillery became the spiritual home of the brand, though its physical contribution was small, especially once Cardhu's

FAR LEFT John Cumming of Cardow, looking every inch the gentleman farmer and showing no trace of his grandfather's nefarious dealings in moonshine. Though Cardow had been sold to John Walker & Sons, Cumming continued to run the distillery.

LEFT Elizabeth Cumming, the first lady distiller on Speyside, who re-equipped Cardow with new stills. The old pair were sold for a few pounds to William Grant who installed them in his new distillery of Glenfiddich.

12-year-old single malt took off in Spain. The Spaniards enjoyed it as a fashionable alternative to Chivas Regal – the country's top-selling deluxe blend. With sales growing by 100,000 cases a year from 1997 to 2002, demand was set to outstrip supply. Rather than raise the price to restrict demand, Cardhu's owners Diageo rechristened the brand Cardhu Pure Malt and blended in malts from neighbouring distilleries. In doing so they provoked a very public spat in the media, cries of betrayal and even questions in the House of Commons. Unleashed from the constraints of being fed from a single distillery, Cardhu could have become the world's most popular malt within 10 years. This fact was not lost on William Grant & Sons, owners of the top-selling malt at the time, Glenfiddich. Together with other distillers they forced Diageo into a humiliating climb-down and Pure Malt was quietly withdrawn from the market in March 2003.

RIGHT Cardhu's license may date from 1824, but its founder John Cumming had been making whisky for a good number of years before then.

BELOW Cardhu as it looks today, with a classic late-Victorian pair of pagoda roofs to draw the smoke from the kiln through the malt.

WHISKY TASTING NOTES
CARDHU 18-YEAR-OLD 40% ABV

There has never been a great deal of Cardhu to spare for bottling as a single malt, due to the seemingly inexorable growth of the Johnnie Walker brand. Cardhu, or Cardow as it was known until 1980, was bought by John Walker & Sons as far back as 1893, and it has been used in its blends ever since.

The official 12-year-old was replaced with the notorious Cardhu Pure Malt in 2003, but reintroduced two years later. More recently there have been a number of older expressions released including this sumptuous, relatively full-bodied 18-year-old that appears to have quite a sherry influence. There is some old leather, macerated fruit and dark chocolate, though still some freshness too.

GLENFARCLAS
BALLINDALLOCH, BANFFSHIRE

ON A MEADOW BENEATH THE BARE, WIND-BLASTED BULK OF BEN RINNES LIES THE FAMILY-OWNED DISTILLERY OF GLENFARCLAS. TO HAVE REMAINED INDEPENDENT WHILE VIRTUALLY EVERY OTHER SCOTTISH DISTILLERY IS IN CORPORATE HANDS IS QUITE AN ACHIEVEMENT. OVER THE YEARS THERE HAVE BEEN UNSOLICITED OFFERS TO BUY GLENFARCLAS, BUT THE GRANT FAMILY ARE RESOLUTELY NOT SELLING.

John Grant took over the tenant farm in 1865 and a small distillery valued at £511 that Robert Hay had founded some 30 years earlier. Grant, a champion breeder of Aberdeen Angus cattle, was probably much more interested in the land than in making whisky. Yet as the demand from the blenders grew for Speyside malt, distilling became more important. The firm of J&G Grant was founded and it was decided that the distillery needed rebuilding. To raise the money a partnership was formed with one of the leading blenders – the Pattison brothers. When Pattison's went spectacularly bust in 1899, Glenfarclas was lucky to survive. The experience seems to have put the Grant's off outside investors for ever. Some "Pure Old Glenfarclas-Glenlivet" malt was bottled, yet the vast

majority went for blending. The whisky baron Tommy Dewar was so moved by Glenfarclas he declared it contained: "The hum of the bee, the hope of Spring, the breath of May ..." and much else besides. In 1925 John Dewar & Sons were paying 6s.3d. a gallon for the whisky, as were John Walker & Sons. With the rest of the industry contracting around it, Glenfarclas must have felt vulnerable until it could establish a name for itself among whisky drinkers through its own single malt. In 1973 much of the distillery was rebuilt into what you see today, with a central hub of buildings surrounded by row upon row of low, old-fashioned, dunnage-style warehouses. That year a visitors' centre was also installed. People traipsed beneath the pagoda roof into a reception room whose panelling came from

BELOW Glenfarclas has remained fiercely independent and wary of partnerships since its last one with the Pattison brothers of Leith went disastrously wrong in 1899.

LEFT There is nothing dainty about the bulky stills at Glenfarclas, but then there's nothing dainty about the whisky either.

WHISKY TASTING NOTES
GLENFARCLAS 105 – 60% ABV

Having very nearly disappeared in the great Pattison crash at the end of the nineteenth century, Glenfarclas has been determined to plough its own furrow as a fiercely independent, family-owned whisky company. From its big, chunky stills flows a spirit that may not be the most subtle on Speyside, but it makes up for it with its generous, full-bodied charm. The 105 is one of the most well-established cask-strength whiskies around, and an undiluted dram is the liquid equivalent of a great bear hug. The full spectrum of sherry aromas waft out, starting with some dusty malt, followed by stewed plums, burnt sugar and chocolate. The palate continues the chocolate theme with more sweet spice from the wood, until eventually this big beast of a whisky fades to a slow finish.

an old luxury liner, the *Empress of Australia*, that was being scrapped. With its years of uninterrupted production and no city investors to placate, Glenfarclas has the luxury of boasting one of the best inventories of aged whisky in the business.

The standard line-up starts with a 10-year-old and progresses right though to the 40-year-old. But for the cask-strength 105 bottling, all the whiskies are in the same-shaped bottle and carry similar labels. What matters to Grant's is the liquid inside rather than any fancy packaging, and by today's inflated prices for rare, old whisky, the 40-year-old is something of a bargain. The style is not dissimilar to the original sherried whiskies of Macallan.

LEFT A few years after Glenfiddich, Glenfarclas opened its visitor centre in 1973 and used panelling from an ocean liner, the *Empress of Australia* that was being scrapped at the time.

BALVENIE
DUFFTOWN, BANFFSHIRE

IT MAY HAVE TAKEN WILLIAM GRANT DECADES TO REALIZE HIS DREAM OF HAVING HIS OWN DISTILLERY OF GLENFIDDICH IN 1887, WITH EVERY PENNY SCRIMPED AND SAVED, BUT IT TOOK HIM JUST FIVE YEARS TO EMBARK ON HIS NEXT PROJECT AT A COST OF £2,000. THE NEW DISTILLERY WAS A CONVERSION OF THE EIGHTEENTH-CENTURY BALVENIE NEW HOUSE, AND ITS STILLS WERE FIRED UP ON 1 MAY 1893.

The decision to build Balvenie was taken partly because Grant had secured a valuable customer – a blender in Aberdeen – from the Glenlivet distillery, which was temporarily closed due to a fire. There was also the fact that a local man had been making enquiries about leasing land next-door to Glenfiddich to establish his own distillery. Had he succeeded he would have been entitled to half of Glenfiddich's precious water supply. To limit the expense, Grant bought his stills second-hand from Lagavulin on Islay and the now defunct Glen Albyn in Inverness. On hearing of a mash-tun for sale that might be too deep, he sent a terse note to his son, dispatching him to take a look. "Don't be afraid of the depth of the mash-tun if otherwise suitable," he wrote. "A man does not need to piss his pot full unless he likes."

At the start of the twentieth century William Grant & Sons was almost brought down by the bankruptcy of the Pattison brothers, one of its main customers. Afterwards it began to focus on its own blends, including "William Grant's Finest" and "Standfast". William Grant died in 1923 and years later one of his daughters-in-law wrote the following about a night-time visit to the distillery: "We would go to the still-house first. There Alfie Mackray, the night still-man, would be making his supper – not a carried 'piece' but a nice, yellow haddock grilled to a turn on a shovel over a clean fire – the furnace fire, and a can, not a flask of tea ..."

The fish suppers may have gone, but Balvenie hasn't

BELOW William Grant's Balvenie is something of a boutique distillery within the grounds of the mighty Glenfiddich which has expanded greatly since the 1960s.

WHISKY TASTING NOTES
BALVENIE 12-YEAR-OLD DOUBLE WOOD
40% ABV

The sister distillery and neighbour to Glenfiddich in Dufftown on Speyside is a very different creature. Balvenie has always been more of a boutique distillery with a loyal following for its finely crafted malts. Double Wood is about taking the malt matured for ten years in ex-bourbon American oak barrels and finishing them in sherry butts, for two years in this case. The richer sherry character may come through more on the tongue and give the whisky its fine creamy texture and add some dark fruit, sweet spice and chocolate to the flavour. On the nose there are some confected fruit aromas, possibly bananas and freshness too. The finish is fresh and tangy.

LEFT Like others, Balvenie has been very inventive with maturation. Its "Triple Cask" range involves ageing in first-fill Bourbon barrels, refill casks and first-fill Oloroso sherry butts.

lost its old-world charm, having retained its floor maltings for a proportion of its malt, so smoke still billows from its pagoda roof. In addition Balvenie remains solidly late Victorian, while thrusting, modern Glenfiddich has expanded all around it. Balvenie eventually released its own single malt in 1973 wrapped in black leatherette and stamped with gold lettering. Quite who it was aimed at is unclear, but the packaging has sobered up since then, and the focus is now very much on wood to emphasize the crafted nature of Balvenie, which still has its own cooperage. As well as the popular Double Wood, there have been releases based on first-fill bourbon barrels, port pipes, rum casks and sherry butts. In 2014 two European oak casks were selected by Balvenie's malt master, David Stewart MBE, for release as a 50-year-old with an eye-popping price tag of £26,000 a bottle.

LEFT Head south from the bustling whisky town of Dufftown, and the scenery grows increasingly dramatic. Before tarmac roads and railways, the region would quickly become cut off behind the granite bulk of the Cairngorms in winter.

CAMPBELTOWN

CUT OFF FROM THE REST OF SCOTLAND AT THE END OF THE A83 WAY DOWN THE MULL OF KINTYRE, IT SEEMS HIGHLY IMPROBABLE THAT CAMPBELTOWN WAS EVER A CENTRE OF WHISKY MAKING. YET IN ITS HEYDAY TOWARDS THE END OF THE NINETEENTH CENTURY, THIS SMALL PORT WAS PUMPING OUT MORE WHISKY THAN ANY OTHER REGION IN SCOTLAND. TODAY IT SEEMS MORE OF A POSTSCRIPT, ALBEIT WITH THE HIGHLY REGARDED INDEPENDENT DISTILLERY OF SPRINGBANK, THE GREAT SURVIVOR ALONG WITH GLEN SCOTIA OF THE WORST DISTILLERY CULL IN THE COUNTRY'S HISTORY. THE RELENTLESS RISE OF CAMPBELTOWN WHISKY MAY HAVE CARRIED WITH IT THE SEEDS OF ITS OWN DEMISE, BUT ITS FALL FROM GRACE WAS SWIFT AND BRUTAL.

THE WHISKY HERITAGE OF CAMPBELTOWN

THANKS TO THE WAY THE MALT WHISKY INDUSTRY GREW UP ON THE FARM AND EVOLVED FROM ILLICIT STILLS SCATTERED ACROSS THE HIGHLANDS, IT HAS ALWAYS APPEARED RURAL AND FAR FLUNG. THE EXCEPTION IS CAMPBELTOWN, AN EPICENTRE OF URBAN DISTILLATION ONCE DUBBED WHISKYOPOLIS. THE TOWN AT THE END OF THE KINTYRE PENINSULA – THE GREAT ARM OF ARGYLL THAT SLIPS SOUTHWARDS INTO THE IRISH SEA – WAS ONCE HOME TO AT LEAST 34 DISTILLERIES.

At one stage before the great late nineteenth-century distillery boom on Speyside, this one town would have been producing more than any whisky region in Scotland. It still had 18 distilleries in operation before the First World War, yet by the end of the 1920s the only one still going was the now long-forgotten Riechlachan. But for the survival of Springbank and Glen Scotia, which reopened in 1934, Campbeltown whisky would have been history.

There was mention of *acquavytie*, or spirit, being delivered to the village of Taylone, 15 miles from Campbeltown, in the late sixteenth century. This is the first written reference, and one can only guess how long the locals were at it before then. It is worth pointing out that the coast of Antrim is just 12 miles away, and that St Columba is said to have stayed here for three years before sailing to Iona in the sixth century.

BELOW Campbeltown had been producing whisky since the early 1600s, if not earlier. By the end of the eighteenth century there were 22 licensed distillers in the town that later became known as "Whiskyopolis".

The Irish like to claim they invented whisky before teaching the Scots how to make it. If so, distilling could have come very early to this remote corner of Argyll.

In 1609 the first licence to produce whisky in the town was granted to John Boyl. The timing was good, for that same year the *Statutes of Icolmkill* had decreed that the Western Highlands should stick to home-made liquor and desist from imported wines and spirits. There were abundant supplies of the two key ingredients – barley and water – and other distillers soon followed. By 1713 whisky making in the town was such that the town council felt the need to appoint three inspectors to ensure no one was producing watered-down whisky, or "insufficient stuff" as it was known. By the end of the century the *Statistical Account* for the Parish of Campbeltown included 22 licensed distilleries, though their annual average production was less than a thousand gallons each.

There was plenty of whisky being made on the side for "domestic consumption", which the authorities eventually banned in 1781. A decade later they effectively drove Campbeltown's licensed distillers underground by raising the licence to an unsustainable £9 per gallon of still capacity. Over the next three years excise officers seized as many as 292 illicit stills in the town. In the years that followed there were several half-hearted measures to try and rekindle the legitimate trade, but it was not until 1817 that anyone in this part of the world could be persuaded to take out a licence. Six years later, the Excise Act finally made legal whisky a worthwhile enterprise, and within little over a decade the number of distilleries in the parish leapt from three to 30. They were well placed to corner the market in Glasgow, having long supplied the city with contraband whisky across the Firth of Clyde. By then Glasgow had overtaken Edinburgh in size and was the fastest-growing city in Britain.

BELOW Freshly-filled casks at Glen Scotia, one of only two survivors — Springbank is the other — of Campbeltown whisky's Victorian heyday.

Some of the new distilleries only lasted a few years, but by the 1870s the numbers had settled on around 20. Nowhere in the world, before or since, has there been such a concentration of distillers in one place. To fire their stills they used coal from the nearby Machrihanish coal seam, while the malt came from 20 local maltsters. Once, when this was just a cottage industry, there had been enough barley grown on the Mull of Kintyre to turn into whisky, but those days had gone. The sheer scale of Campbeltown whisky meant sourcing grain from the Lowlands, Ireland and even Denmark and Russia.

WATCHING THE SPIRIT FLOW

It was said that when one of the Baltic grain ships was in dock every horse and cart in the town had to be requisitioned. "There is no saying where Campbeltown whisky ends, or what it sets in motion as it flows along," wrote the editor of the local paper, "but the volume ... [is] enough to cause a navy as well as men's heads to swim." To cope with all the by-products of their whisky making, the distillers had to set up a special plant to process them. Wet grains and draff were sold locally at 4d. a bushel, while dried grains were reportedly shipped to Rotterdam to feed the horses of the German army.

By 1886 production was estimated at over 2.6 million proof gallons, and it was claimed that Campbeltown with its two thousand citizens had the highest income per capita of any town in Britain. Its whisky barons, such as the Colvilles, Mitchells and Fergusons, built themselves opulent villas on the east side of the town where they could watch the endless flow of spirit down Campbeltown Loch to the blenders in Glasgow. Any that wondered whether it was too good to last, didn't have to wait long.

There were rumours, perhaps spread by other whisky regions, that the town's distillers had grown complacent and were content to use old herring barrels to store their whiskies. It is true the big blending houses were turning away from the smoky, oily style of Campbeltown in favour of Speyside, but the real reason for the town's decline can be found in the storms buffeting the entire industry. There was the slump after the speculative late-Victorian boom, followed by cut-backs during the war and steep hikes in excise tax in 1918 and 1920. Then came American Prohibition and the Depression. When the Scotch whisky industry finally recovered it was very different, because the town's myriad independent distilleries no longer fitted in.

Yet all is not lost, and out of the ashes of Whiskyopolis, three distilleries have survived, including the iconic Springbank, doing its best to keep Campbeltown on the map.

OPPOSITE A modern-style racked warehouse at Glen Scotia.

BELOW The calm waters of Campbeltown Loch would have once been disturbed by an endless flow of spirit, but almost all the town's distillers disappeared thanks to the early twentieth-century whisky slump and US Prohibition.

SPRINGBANK AND CAMPBELTOWN'S OTHER SURVIVING DISTILLERIES
KINTYRE, ARGYLL & BUTE

IN 1828, CAMPBELTOWN GOT ITS 14TH LICENSED DISTILLERY IN THE SHAPE OF SPRINGBANK. IT WAS BUILT ON THE SITE OF SOME OLD MALT BARNS IN THE CENTRE OF TOWN THAT BELONGED TO ARCHIBALD MITCHELL.

As a maltster supplying all the new distilleries that were springing up, Mitchell was evidently making whisky on the side, judging by the ledger of a local firm of coppersmiths who were supplying him with the necessary kit. The Springbank distillery was actually established by his in-laws – the Reid family – but they soon found themselves in financial difficulties and the distillery was taken over by Archibald's two youngest sons, John and William Mitchell, in 1837. Within a year the reputation of the whisky had spread as far as Kilmarnock and a young grocer called John Walker who bought a quantity for 8s.8d. a gallon. It was a nice early endorsement from the man who would eventually lend his name to the world's best-elling Scotch, although the amount he paid when adjusted for inflation wouldn't even cover the duty today.

At some stage the brothers fell out over their other activity, sheep farming, and William Mitchell left to become a founding partner in Rieclachan – the town's last distillery to close for good in 1934. He later went on to establish Glengyle in 1872, by which point the extended Mitchell family had interests in four distilleries. Of these, Springbank, which traded under the name J&A Mitchell & Co. Ltd, was by far the largest.

BELOW Long before today's whisky anoraks began bagging remote distilleries, there was Alfred Barnard. During the 1880s he visited every single one of them for his seminal work: *The Whisky Distilleries of the United Kingdom.*

ABOVE Barnard would have been amazed that so many Campbeltown distilleries disappeared, and that Springbank was one of just two survivors. With its direct-fired stills and floor maltings it remains one of the most traditional.

When the Victorian whisky writer Alfred Barnard visited Campbeltown in the 1870s he wrote that "in former times the only trade of the place was herring fishing, net making and smuggling". By the time he got there it was definitely a one-industry town with 21 distilleries, all of which he visited. Having waxed lyrical about Hazelburn, the town's biggest distillery, he descended on Springbank with his notebook in hand. Every detail from the capacity of each washback, to the diameter of the boiler, and the horse-power of the steam engine was duly recorded, including the distillery's annual output. This was put at 145,000 gallons of "Campbeltown Malt" which was "principally sold in London and Glasgow". Barnard then progressed to Dalintober, Benmore and a host of other long-lost distilleries. There is not the slightest hint that Springbank might be one of the very few survivors.

SURVIVAL INSTINCT

More remarkable is the fact that Springbank has remained in the same family's hands since 1828, longer than any other distillery in Scotland. Yet that same sense of grim determination to remain independent when ownership of almost the entire industry is now shared by a few corporate players, may be a clue to its survival. Above all Springbank is a remarkably self-contained operation from start to finish. The original floor maltings are used to malt the barley, while the spirit is matured in the distillery's own warehouses on site. Even the bottling of the finished whisky is done at Springbank.

All this is relatively recent. Back in the 1980s Springbank was buying in its malted barley and sending its whisky off for blending like virtually every malt distillery in Scotland. Having just the one distillery down the far end of the Kintyre peninsula, left the firm of J&A Mitchell particularly vulnerable to any downturn in the industry. With their warehouses full of whisky in search of a home, the big blenders lost interest in the early 1980s. They were too busy closing their own distilleries to worry about

ABOVE One set of stills, but three distinct malts including triple distilled, unpeated Hazelburn and robust, smoky Longrow which were both distilleries in their own right once upon a time.

buying in outside stock. Springbank desperately needed to control its own fate, and would have perished but for the great malt renaissance pioneered by Glenfiddich in the 1960s. If single malt was to be the saviour, the methods used were to be as traditional as possible. In 1992, the family decided to restore the old floor maltings and fire up the kilns with peat from Tomintoul. At the same time they determined that no more fillings would be sold to blenders, and to expand Springbanks's repertoire of malts under the names of Hazelburn and Longrow – two of the town's erstwhile distilleries. Hazelburn is triple distilled from unpeated malt and then part matured in sherry casks in the case of the 12-year-old, while Longrow is double distilled and distinctly smoky. Springbank sits neatly in the middle with moderately peated barley that is distilled two and a half times.

By 2000 Springbank had developed something of a cult following among single malt enthusiasts, and Hedley Wright decided to buy the distillery next door, founded by his ancestor William Mitchell in 1872. But for an empty shell there was not much left of Glengyle, which had not produced a drop of whisky for eighty years. Two second-hand pot stills were bought from Ben Wyvis – a malt distillery within the giant Invergordon grain distillery. After some slight modifications to improve the reflux, or copper contact between the spirit and the still, a lightly peated whisky was produced under the name Kilkerran.

It could not be called Glengyle because that name belongs to Campbeltown's third surviving distillery – Glen Scotia. Originally called Scotia it was established in 1832 by Stewart Galbraith & Co. Alfred Barnard wrote that it "seems to have hidden its way out of sight, as if the art of making Whisky, at that time, was bound to be kept a dark secret". In 1930, the then owner Duncan MacCallum threw himself into Campbeltown Loch after a dodgy business deal went wrong. His ghost still haunts the still-room, or so they say.

After a brief spell with the Bloch brothers, who cannot have found Campbeltown too convenient, given their other distillery was on Orkney, Glen Scotia eventually ended up with Glen Catrine (Loch Lomond Distillers) in 1994. It had undergone a £1 million refurbishment in the 1970s, but had spent many of the subsequent years in mothballs. Having brought the two stills back to life, the new owners have managed to bring out various aged expressions including a 12- and a 14-year-old despite the gaping holes in the inventory. The distillery has long been in the shadow of Springbank, but maybe it will start to emerge now that the parent company, Glen Catrine, has been bought by a private equity company as part of a management buy-out.

BELOW A sea of recently disgorged barrels await their next filling of new-make spirit of Springbank, Hazelburn and Longrow.

WHISKY TASTING NOTES
SPRINGBANK 15-YEAR-OLD 46% ABV

The great survivor down in Campbeltown and one of the few independents left in the industry, Springbank has a loyal following among malt whisky aficionados. The distillery rewards its fans with consistently good bottlings, setting the bar high with its entry level 10 year old. The house style is generous, robust and slightly salty. This older expression is a big beefy whisky with a distinct sherry influence. The nose is complex and offers candied fruit, toffee, coconut and some exotic sweet and sour spice. On the tongue the toffee and dried fruit notes continue, but this is balanced by dry spice, a little sea spray and some smoke as well. Adding a drop of water seems to smooth out the texture and enhance those fruit flavours.

BELOW Since it was built in 1832 by Stewart, Glabraith & Co, Glen Scotia has changed hands nine times. Its current owner, since 1994, is Loch Lomond Distillers.

ABOVE Despite being one of Scotland's smallest distilleries, Glen Scotia still manages to produce three very different whiskies from unpeated to heavily peated.

THE LOWLANDS

DISTILLING WAS ONCE AS ENDEMIC IN THE LOWLANDS AS IT WAS IN THE HIGHLANDS. THERE WERE A HANDFUL OF BIG, COMMERCIAL DISTILLERIES PUMPING OUT WHISKY AT A FEROCIOUS PACE, AND ENDLESS ILLICIT STILLS OPERATING EVERYWHERE FROM REMOTE FARMSTEADS TO INNER-CITY TENEMENTS. THE RISK OF BEING CAUGHT MAY HAVE BEEN GREATER THAN IN THE HIGHLANDS AND ISLANDS, BUT ACCESS TO THE MARKET AND GOOD-QUALITY GRAIN WOULD HAVE BEEN MUCH BETTER. YET THANKS TO IMPROVED TRANSPORT THOSE BENEFITS HAVE FADED, AND OTHER MARKETABLE QUALITIES LIKE HAVING A ROMANTIC LOCATION HAVE COME TO THE FORE. TODAY THE LOWLANDS DOMINATE GRAIN WHISKY PRODUCTION, BUT MALT DISTILLERIES ARE FEW AND FAR BETWEEN.

THE WHISKY HERITAGE OF THE LOWLANDS

OVER THE PAST 150 YEARS TRAINS, PLANES AND AUTOMOBILES HAVE SHRUNK SCOTLAND AND MADE IT FAR MORE ACCESSIBLE. TODAY YOU CAN DRIVE THE 200-ODD MILES FROM EDINBURGH TO ULLAPOOL IN SUTHERLAND — THE GATEWAY TO THE OUTER HEBRIDES — IN A LITTLE OVER FOUR HOURS. BEFORE THE INVENTION OF TARMAC HOWEVER, IT WOULD HAVE TAKEN DAYS. IT WOULD HAVE BEEN A HUGE JOURNEY AND PROBABLY BEST AVOIDED IN WINTER WHEN SNOW AND ICE WOULD HAVE OFTEN BLOCKED ALL ROUTES TO THE NORTH.

More to the point there would have been little incentive to stray far from that great beacon of the Enlightenment, Edinburgh, and venture into the dim twilight zone of the Highlands with its feudal chieftains and warlike clans. This was before the region was romanticized into the "land of the mountain and the flood" by Sir Walter Scott – previously its people had been seen as barbarians. Scott's bestselling novels, and more specifically his stage managing of George IV's famous state visit to Edinburgh in 1822, changed for ever the way Scotland saw itself and was perceived by others.

Before then the Highland boundary fault, said to be visible from space, signified a cultural fault line as well. In the Lowlands, particularly in Central Belt farmland and along the East Coast, the agricultural revolution was transforming the land. Thanks to better crop rotation, improved ploughing methods, the advent of new fertilizers and proper drainage, yields from the region's arable farms improved dramatically. More grain per acre boosted production for the Lowland whisky barons like the Steins.

It was probably in the 1720s that Andrew Stein built the Kennetpans distillery near Alloa, which was soon vying with Ferintosh on the Black Isle for the title of Scotland's largest distillery. Stein also founded a great whisky dynasty which included the Haigs and stretched to Dublin, where John Stein established the Bow Street distillery which became home to Jameson's whiskey. In 1786, the Steins installed one of James Watt's first ever steam engines at Kennetpans, having established the giant Kilbaggie distillery nearby, which was really the first to export whisky. It was sent to England in bulk for rectifying into gin.

This sparked off a bitter war with the London distillers and those that supplied them. Being closer to Parliament and perhaps with deeper pockets to bribe politicians, they managed to choke off the competition from the north. The Steins, whose five distilleries were responsible for half the legalized whisky in Scotland,

BELOW Raymond Armstrong (in the red shirt) admiring a cask sample of Bladnoch, the Lowland distillery he rescued in 1994. Sadly, despite his best efforts, it went into liquidation 20 years later.

BOTTOM The Bladnoch bridge by the Galloway village of Bladnoch which in its Victorian prime boasted three grocers' shops, an iron foundry, a creamery, a coach-building business, two inns, a tailor, a potato mill and a distillery.

went bust, and the Lowlands were flooded with cheap raw spirit masquerading as whisky. The family did manage to bounce back for a while with Cameronbridge in Fife, where Robert Stein designed and installed Scotland's first continuous still in 1828. It became the prototype for Aeneas Coffey's patent still two years later.

Clearly not all Lowland distilling was done on an industrial scale or aimed principally at the insatiable London gin market. There were over 200 licensed distilleries here by the end of the eighteenth century, the vast majority producing malt whisky in small pot stills. There was also a thriving trade in moonshine produced on farms and in smuggling hotspots like the Campsie Fells north of Glasgow. Of course, before long, smugglers in the Lowlands needed to be more circumspect than those in the Highlands, where there were far fewer excisemen about. In fact, it may well have been easier to escape detection in town. In Edinburgh a gauger would have needed a very good

nose to pick up fumes of illicit whisky amid the coal-fired stench of Auld Reekie, as the city was known.

FEELING THE PINCH

After the whisky industry came of age in the 1820s and farm distilleries took out licences and became commercial enterprises, Lowland whisky was gradually eclipsed by other regions. The big blending houses looked first to Campbeltown and then to Speyside to provide the bulk of their blends. The likes of Glenlivet were imbued with a Highland romance that no Lowland distillery could ever match. A century later, when distilleries began to bottle and actively promote their own malts led by Glenfiddich and others on Speyside, the Lowlands slipped further off the radar. Single malts were perceived as the spirit of the Highlands and Islands, where each whisky reflected its rugged and remote setting. In a word, there was something too mundane about the Central Belt, although you could hardly say that about the Scottish

BELOW The Grange distillery in Burntisland, Fife was founded by Andrew Philp in 1786, and operated on and off until its final closure in 1927.

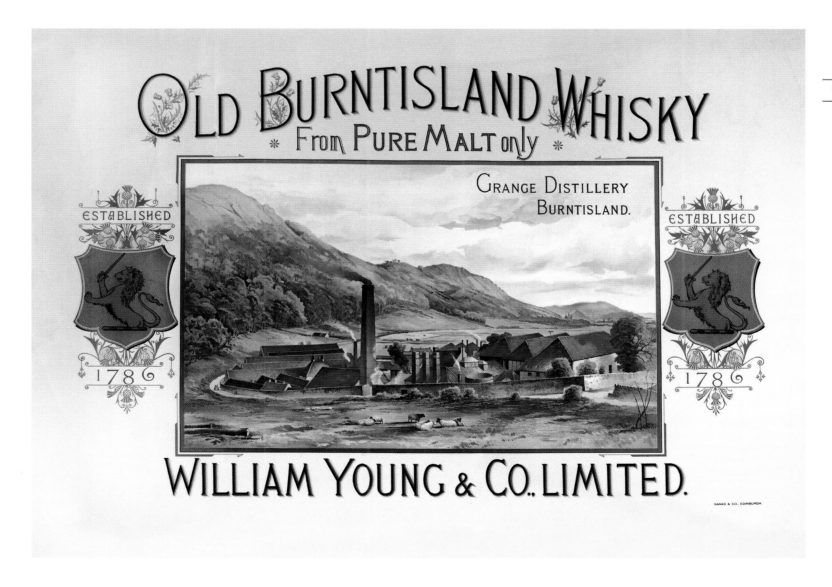

OLD BURNTISLAND WHISKY
* From Pure Malt only *

GRANGE DISTILLERY
BURNTISLAND.

ESTABLISHED 1786

ESTABLISHED 1786

WILLIAM YOUNG & CO., LIMITED.

Borders or swathes of Dumfries, which can be every bit as wild and beautiful as further north.

Today, there are really just two survivors among Lowland malt distilleries from the nineteenth century – Auchentoshan, out west of Glasgow, founded in 1800, and Glenkinchie, established 37 years later, south-east of Edinburgh. At the time of writing, a question mark hung over the region's only other nineteenth-century malt distillery – Bladnoch, in Dumfries, that was founded in 1817 by Thomas McClelland. It remained in family hands for over a century and was then passed around until finally ending up with United Distillers. In the early 1990s it was considered too small and remote and was closed down. Bladnoch was then saved by Raymond Armstrong, who ran it as a boutique distillery producing just 100,000 litres a year before being forced into liquidation in 2014.

In recent years there were a few other Lowland survivors like Rosebank and St Magdalene, though if mothballed they were always more vulnerable to a downturn in the industry than some far-flung Highland distillery. Rosebank in Falkirk was redeveloped into flats after it closed in 1993. Had it been in Wester Ross it might well have survived. But what the Lowlands lack in malt whisky production is more than made up for in grain. Add together the grain whisky from Girvan in Ayrshire, Strathclyde in Glasgow, North British in Edinburgh and the giant Cameronbridge in Fife, and it would easily eclipse all the malt whisky produced in Scotland. And not all the spirit disappears into blends, as demonstrated by Diageo's new, David Beckham-endorsed Haig Club whisky in its fancy blue bottle. It may be coy about its provenance, but every drop of this single-grain whisky is distilled at Cameronbridge.

If other grain distillers were to copy the idea and try and build their own mainstream brands of grain whisky it could transform Lowland whisky-making. So far this has not happened and what expressions there are currently available have tended to be more at the top-end of the market like the Patent Still single grain releases from William Grant's Girvan distillery in Ayrshire, or the so-called "G-spot" bottles from the Scotch Malt Whisky Society.

OPPOSITE A poster from 1937 advertising what was then Britain's favourite Scotch. Today the brand is probably best-known for its recently launched Haig Club grain whisky that is promoted by a certain David Beckham.

BELOW In the past distilleries had their own excise officers who would record the weight of each filled cask before it was rolled into a bonded warehouse. A two per cent loss through evaporation – the so-called angel's share – was allowed each year.

GLENKINCHIE
PENCAITLAND, EAST LOTHIAN

WHEN JOHN AND GEORGE RATE TOOK UP DISTILLING WHISKY ON THEIR EAST LOTHIAN FARM IN 1825, THEY DID NOT HAVE TO LOOK FAR FOR THEIR RAW INGREDIENTS. THE RICH ALLUVIAL SOIL MAKES THIS PRIME BARLEY-GROWING COUNTRY, AND THERE WAS WATER FROM THE KINCHIE BURN TO MAKE THE MASH. WITH A BURGEONING MARKET IN EDINBURGH JUST FIFTEEN MILES AWAY, THE SMALL DISTILLERY APPEARED PERFECTLY PLACED. THERE WAS EVEN A RAILWAY DIRECT TO THE CITY CENTRE WHOSE TRACKS RAN JUST A FEW HUNDRED YARDS FROM THE DISTILLERY. BUT SOMETHING HAPPENED CAUSING THE RATES TO SELL UP IN 1853.

Then came the boom in blended Scotch, and with demand spreading to England and beyond, the prospects for Glenkinchie began to look up. As readers of the *Wine Trade Review* discovered in 1886: "The future of the wine trade is whisky." Up in Edinburgh it seems they already knew that, for five years earlier a consortium of various wine merchants and a local brewer decided to set up The Glen Kinchie

Distillery Co. The stills were fired back into life to provide malt for the blends, particularly Haig's Gold Label and Dimple. The distillery was later licensed to John Haig & Co.

The new owners completely rebuilt Glenkinchie into what you see today – a relatively substantial, four-storey distillery in red brick. It has a functional, somewhat municipal feel about it, but it was clearly

BELOW Every malt distillery has a locked spirit's safe through which the new-make spirit flows. Once the initial foreshots have come through, the distiller starts to collect the middle cut before rejecting the feints at the end.

WHISKY TASTING NOTES
GLENKINCHIE 2000 DISTILLER'S EDITION 43% ABV

If you have spent too long on Islay, and been seduced by its hairy collection of peat monsters, Glenkinchie might seem rather tame and perhaps, to some smokeheads, not even whisky at all. The counter argument might be that this Lowland distillery south of Edinburgh is all about subtlety and nuance. Better still, people should try this Distiller's Edition malt which has been rounded off at the end of maturation in Amontillado sherry casks, and decide for themselves. It has Glenkinchie's classic lightness of touch and dry grassy aroma, sweetened with the sherry oak. The palate is brisk and dry with a big hit of malt that fades to a lingering finish.

efficient. In no time its pair of old pot stills, among the biggest in the industry, were pumping out almost 80,000 gallons of spirit a year. This was filled into casks and then dispatched via a siding onto the railway line to Edinburgh. The distillery even had its own overhead railway system to carry the grain to the floor maltings. Once malted, it was crushed in the grist hopper and transported by a mechanical elevator to a mash tun complete with mechanically powered rakes. By comparison with a typical Highland malt distillery at the time, Glenkinchie was positively space-age.

In 1914, it became part of a group of Lowland malt distilleries that was swallowed up by the Distillers Company after the First World War. During the next war, Glenkinchie was almost unique in being allowed to continue distillation every year, albeit at a much reduced rate. In 1969, the old floor maltings were converted into a museum, which may have played a small part in its owners' decision to pick the distillery to represent the Lowlands in its original line-up of six Classic Malts launched in 1988. The other contender was Rosebank in Falkirk whose whisky was possibly more esteemed, so maybe Glenkinchie was lucky to survive.

Being the closest distillery to Edinburgh it receives a steady stream of visitors from the capital.

ABOVE Glenkincchie is surrounded by rich, arable farmland, part of the East Coast barley belt that stretches from the Black Isle to the Borders.

BELOW Behind its red brick façade, Glenkinchie was one of the most modern and heavily automated distilleries in the country.

AUCHENTOSHAN
CLYDEBANK, WEST DUNBARTONSHIRE

SCOTLAND'S OTHER MAIN LOWLAND DISTILLERY LIES CLOSE TO THE CLYDE, SOME TEN MILES DOWNSTREAM OF GLASGOW. IT WAS FOUNDED IN 1800 BY THE VILLAGE OF OLD KIRKPATRICK AND SEEMS TO HAVE BEEN ORIGINALLY KNOWN AS DUNTOCHER BEFORE IT BECAME AUCHENTOSHAN. BACK THEN IT WAS OPEN COUNTRY, WHEREAS TODAY THE FIELDS HAVE BEEN SWALLOWED UP BY THE URBAN SPRAWL OF GLASGOW AND ITS SUBURBS SPREADING WESTWARDS.

The first mention of "Auchentoshan" – meaning "corner of the field" – is from 1649 and refers to a monastery that would have been dissolved the previous century. The monks would have almost certainly brewed their own beer, and if they went further and distilled it, then the roots of whisky making here may be very old, though this is pure conjecture. What we do know is that Auchentoshan was like a small Highland farm distillery, and in a similar way only took out a licence in 1825 after a good two decades of making moonshine. It was first owned by a man named Thorne, who was followed by the

BELOW Auchentoshan, Scotland's other surviving Lowland malt distillery, is part of a stable of Scotch whiskies including Bowmore, Ardmore, Glen Garioch and Teachers owned by Japanese parent company, Beam Suntory.

BELOW Auchentoshan, Scotland's other surviving Lowland malt distillery, is part of a stable of Scotch whiskies including Bowmore, Ardmore, Glen Garioch and Teachers owned by Japanese parent company, Beam Suntory.

Filshie family and then the firm of CH Curtis in Greenock. It was they who showed Alfred Barnard round on his great distillery tour of the 1880s. In his book, Barnard describes Auchentoshan as a "little distillery ... situated in a romantic glen with a stream of water running past it". He adds that "at the time of our visit the haymakers were busy in the fields connected with the Distillery and consequently the Works were almost abandoned."

From a whisky point of view what sets Auchentoshan apart is the fact the spirit is triple distilled like Irish whiskey. A middle still sits between the wash and the spirit still to help separate the heads and tails and produce a cleaner, more refined spirit. Triple distillation gives you a lower yield and a higher alcoholic strength. People have speculated that Auchentoshan was simply playing to Glasgow's large Irish population who wanted a taste of home. On the other hand, triple distillation was once remarkably common in Lowland distilleries lying far from any Irish community. During the Clydeside blitz, on 13 March 1940, the Luftwaffe scored a direct hit on one of Auchentoshan's warehouses causing the loss of 53 butts of whisky. In the 1980s, having been owned by various brewers including Tennent's, it was sold to Morrison Bowmore, who in turn were swallowed up by the Japanese drinks giant Suntory. Now that Suntory own Jim Beam, Auchentoshan sits in the same stable as Teachers, Ardmore, Glen Garioch and Bowmore.

ABOVE Checking the spirit safe at Auchentoshan, the closest distillery to Glasgow's and famed for its Irish-style triple distillation.

BELOW Auchentoshan made headlines in 1941 when one of its warehouses received a direct hit from a bomb during the Clyde Blitz, sending a flaming stream of whisky into the river. The bomb crater was later turned into the distillery pond.

WHISKY TASTING NOTES
AUCHENTOSHAN THREE WOOD EDITION
43% ABV

As one of just two survivors among old Lowland malt distilleries, Auchentoshan produces a light, grassy whisky which is made even more gentle through triple distillation in the Irish style. On to this pale canvas is painted a riot of sherry flavours in "Three Wood" which involves maturation in ex-Oloroso and Pedro Ximenez casks, as well as some American oak bourbon barrels. There is lots of dried fruit and burnt sugar on the whisky's fragrant nose, which gives way to a syrupy, mouth-filling palate. There are flavours of dried figs, raisins, dark chocolate and toffee which continue to the finish, though whether you can really taste the subtle distillery character of Auchentoshan beneath that sherried oak is a moot point.

PART THREE

WHISKY CULTURE AND TRADITIONS

BURNS NIGHT AND HOGMANAY

BURNS NIGHT, AS EVERYONE KNOWS, IS WHISKY NIGHT — A BACCHANALIAN FEAST TO CELEBRATE THE NATIONAL BARD'S BIRTHDAY ON 25 JANUARY. AS ONE DRAM LURCHES INTO ANOTHER IN AN UNSTEADY PROCESSION OF TOASTS, A POOR, DEFENCELESS HAGGIS IS SACRIFICED — ITS BELLY SLASHED OPEN TO REVEAL ITS "GUSHING ENTRAILS BRIGHT". THIS BEING A LINE FROM BURNS'S ADDRESS "TO A HAGGIS" WHICH IS ALWAYS RECITED IN ROUSING TONES BY THE MASTER OF CEREMONIES AS HE WIELDS THE KNIFE.

In 1801, five years after Robert Burns died, a group of his friends met in the cottage where he was born in the Ayrshire village of Alloway for the first ever Burns supper. With haggis, poetry, singing and doubtless plenty of whisky, the evening was a great success and the friends decided to make it an annual event. A year later merchants in Greenock hosted the first Burns Club supper, and the idea was quickly adopted by other West Coast towns with a connection to the poet.

By 1806 Burns Night had reached Oxford University and four years later London. It then spread overseas when Scottish army officers celebrated the first Burns supper in India in 1812. Similar haggis and whisky-fuelled celebrations were reported in Canada, and before long the night had become a regular fixture in the calendar for ex-pat Scots throughout the Empire. In the furthest-flung tea estate or jute mill they may have struggled to find a haggis every year, but the drink was surely always whisky.

The combination of whisky and haggis is no accident. Haggis is made from sheep's pluck (heart, liver and lungs), minced up with oatmeal, spices and suet, wrapped in sausage casing and simmered for a few hours. It tastes better than it sounds! "It's a very democratic dish," says Jo Macsween, joint MD of the famous family-run haggis business. "It's a poor man's feast made from humble ingredients that fills you up. It's not about airs and graces which is good symbolism for a man of the earth who rose to meteoric literary fame within his own lifetime." Whether or not it was Burns's favourite dish, he clearly enjoyed rubbing the genteel noses of Edinburgh society in those gushing entrails "warm-reekin rich!"

LEFT Edinburgh's spectacular fireworks display over the Castle is the climax of its Hogmanay celebrations which double the city's population and pump millions into the local economy.

THE FIRST FOOT.

ENTER MR. PUNCH, WHO WISHES EVERYONE "A MERRY CHRISTMAS AND A HAPPY NEW YEAR!"

"The first foot in a house brings good or ill-luck for the year."—*Old Belief.*

ABOVE First footing, or visiting friends and neighbours after midnight on New Year's Eve, still goes on. To ensure good luck the first visitor should be a dark male, as opposed to a blonde Viking, and carry a lump of coal or a black bun.

Whisky is the perfect partner not least because its fiery flavours cut through the fat and spice of the dish far better than any wine – a drink that Burns has fun dismissing for its fancy ways in the opening lines of his epic ode to "Scotch Drink": "Let other poets raise a fracas Bout vines, an' wines, an' drucken Bacchus." Yet more than this, the real appeal is the honest, homespun nature of whisky, whose ingredients and origins are every bit as humble as haggis. Admittedly this may have been obscured somewhat by the way Scotch whisky is now priced and promoted, but in Burns's day it was a very earthy spirit indeed. He was certainly fond of a dram, as much for its effect as its taste, as the following line in the same poem makes clear: "But oil'd by thee, the wheels o' life gae down-hill, scrievin, Wi' rattlin glee!"

"Scotch Drink", written in 1785, sees Burns confessing to his muse – good Scots ale and particularly whisky.

O Whisky! soul o' plays and pranks!
Accept a bardie's gratfu' thanks!
When wanting thee, what tuneless cranks
Are my poor verses!
Thou comes – they rattle in their ranks,
At ither's arses!

The poem continues with a lament for the loss of Ferintosh, Scotland's first true commercial distillery on the Black Isle near Inverness, and then pours scorn on the "curst horse-leeches o' the' Excise". This was somewhat ironic given that Burns became an excise officer four years later in Dumfries. He spent his last eight years in the job, covering large tracts of the county on horse to ensure duty was paid on everything from candles and soap to tea and tobacco. There are no records of him involved with any

BELOW No Burns Night would be complete without the ritual disembowelling of the haggis. For Burns, the dish shared all the humble homespun goodness of whisky.

distillery in the area, though he did apprehend at least one farmer for making moonshine on the side. It also inspired his poem "The De'il's Awa' Wi' th' Exciseman", written in 1792.

The long, damp days in the saddle may have hastened his demise, and Robert Burns died on 21 July 1796, aged 37. His total assets were valued at a mere £200, which scarcely reflects his current value to the Scottish economy. In 2009 the accountant turned comedian Fred MacAuley estimated that "Burns the brand" was worth £160 million a year. He also revealed that the biggest seller by far at the Tam O'Shanter Experience gift shop in Alloway was not the Isle of Arran single malt – the only whisky endorsed by the World Burns Federation. Nor was it postcards, tea-towels or even books of his poems. It was in fact the Rabbie Burns fridge magnet.

The tacky souvenirs may outsell bottles of whisky, but according to one report by an economist at the World Bank in 2003, global sales of Scotch jump 2 per cent on the night, which speaks for itself.

LEFT Rabbie Burns, the national bard, whose self-confessed muse was Scotch whisky, the only conceivable drink to wash down some haggis on his birthday on 25 January.

BELOW The haggis, or "Great chieftain o' the pudding-race!", to quote Burns, is traditionally piped in. Having been addressed by the master of ceremonies it is then disembowelled on the end of a sharp knife.

WHISKY IN POPULAR CULTURE

SIR HARRY LAUDER WAS THE BILLY CONNOLLY OF HIS DAY, ONLY FAR MORE SUCCESSFUL. IN A FORTY-YEAR CAREER IN VAUDEVILLE AND MUSIC HALL, HE HAD BECOME THE WORLD'S HIGHEST-PAID PERFORMER BY 1911 AND WAS THE FIRST SCOTTISH ARTIST TO SELL A MILLION RECORDS. ACCORDING TO SIR WINSTON CHURCHILL HE WAS "SCOTLAND'S GREATEST EVER AMBASSADOR" — ALTHOUGH MANY SCOTS MIGHT DISPUTE THAT TODAY, FEELING MORE AFFINITY WITH BILLY CONNOLLY THAN A SENTIMENTAL OLD CLOWN IN A KILT.

Born in 1870 in Edinburgh's Portobello, Lauder turned professional in his early twenties and soon had his name in lights above the London Pavilion and other leading music halls. As well as "Roamin' in the Gloamin" and "I Love a Lassie", his hits included "A Wee Deoch an Doris". This is Gaelic for a farewell dram – the sort of drink that leads to another, which is fine so long as you can manage the tongue-twister at the end of the chorus:

Just a wee deoch an doris, just a wee drop, that's all.
Just a wee deoch an doris afore ye gang awa.
There's a wee wifie waitin' in a wee but an ben.
If you can say, "It's a braw bricht moonlicht nicht",
Then yer a'richt, ye ken.

Like his kilt and trademark corkscrew walking stick, Scotch was one of Lauder's props in portraying the comic, drunken Scot – an image that featured in many an Edwardian whisky advert. And, with his 22 tours of America, he may have fostered the idea that if you were not in a kilt, clutching a bottle and swaying gently in the breeze, then you probably weren't Scottish at all. He was knighted for all his fund-raising activities in the First World War, and was close friends with the grocery tycoon Sir Thomas Lipton and the whisky baron Tommy Dewar.

In 1897 Dewar's was the subject of possibly the first advertising film ever made. Produced by Thomas Edison and associates, it featured four actors who appeared to have raided the dressing-up box for items including a dinner jacket, bearskin, spear and shield. They are all in kilts, one absurdly short, one back to front, and end by dancing a drunken Highland fling in front of a banner for Dewar's White Label. A version for the English market, "Spirit of his Ancestors", was filmed four years later, and had the four kilted men raising a toast to Queen Victoria.

HARRY LAUDER

I LOVE A LASSIE, A BONNIE, BONNIE LASSIE,
SHE'S AS PURE AS THE LILY IN THE DELL
SHE'S AS SWEET AS THE HEATHER, THE BONNIE, BLOOMIN' HEATHER
MARY, MA SCOTCH BLUEBELL.

Charges to pay

_____ s. _____ d.

RECEIVED

At _____ m

From

By

POST OFFICE

TELEGRAM

| Prefix. | Time handed in. | Office of Origin and Service Instructions. | Words. |

34

No. _____

OFFICE STAMP

CONFIRMATION

ELGIN
9 MAY 1947

At _____ m

To

By

34 C CW AGW 245 GBW 2039 QRC

759 CHICAGO ILL 36 8 1409 =

NLT THE GLENLIVET DISTILLERY GLENLIVET BALLINDALLOCH

= IN OUR EFFORTS TO RETURN TO PREWAR SERVICES WE

DESIRE GLENLIVET SCOTCH TWO OUNCE MINIATURES ARE

YOU IN POSITION TO SUPPLY AND HOW SOON =

THE PULLMAN COMPANY L C ARMFIELD +

G.N.P.Co. Ltd.   51-8490.

For free repetition of doubtful words telephone "TELEGRAMS ENQUIRY" or call, with this form at office of delivery. Other enquiries should be accompanied by this form, and, if possible, the envelope.

B or C

ABOVE With help from Hollywood, the US became Scotch whisky's biggest export market after the war, and distilleries like Glenlivet could barely keep pace with demand as per this telegram from the Pullman Company.

RIGHT The film *Whisky Galore!* was no sentimental, soft-focus portrayal of Hebridean life during wartime. It was more a riotous celebration of whisky and the islanders' ingenuity at beating the system.

OPPOSITE Whisky was one of Sir Harry Lauder's chief props along with his kilt, feathered bonnet and knobbly walking stick. It was not the most subtle of national stereotypes.

PROBLEMS WITH PROHIBITION

Before long Scotch whisky was appearing on the big screen, although once Prohibition began, drinking scenes were no longer shown. According to Daniel Okrent in his book *Last Call*, Hollywood initially supported the ban, believing that if people were denied access to the saloon they would flock to the movies. That soon changed, and in a survey of 115 films released in 1929, Okrent found that drinking was depicted in two-thirds of them, "more often than not favourably".

In 1949 London's Ealing Studios released the ultimate whisky film – *Whisky Galore!* – about a Hebridean island community who are saved from a prolonged whisky drought by a shipwreck laden with Scotch. Based on Compton Mackenzie's book, which fictionalized the tale of the actual sinking of the SS *Politician* off Eriskay in 1941, the film was directed by Alexander Mackendrick and stars Joan Greenwood, Basil Rathbone, Gordon Jackson and James Robertson Justice. On the eve of its re-release in 2011, *The Independent*'s film critic, Jonathan Romney, wrote that it "stands out as depicting Scottish island culture in a no-nonsense, caricature-free fashion". He added that "modern viewers may be surprised to see how enthusiastically pro-booze

Whisky Galore! is. It's a celebration of what, the film reminds us, comes from the Gaelic *uisge beatha* – the water of life."

The film was a hit in the States as *Tight Little Island*, and also in France, where its title *Whisky à Go-Go* inspired dozens of whisky bars to spring up. In both countries it fed a real fondness for the land of Scotch. Deluxe blends like Chivas Regal came to symbolize success and status in post-war America, and this image was re-exported by Hollywood to the rest of the world. Visions of glamorous film stars, with a cigarette in one hand and a Scotch in the other, boosted global tobacco and whisky sales no end.

BELOW LEFT Eddie Izzard stars as the pompous and irredeemably English Captain Waggett in the 2017 remake of the original Ealing comedy. The critics were not entirely convinced.

BELOW A dead serious Daniel Craig as James Bond in 2012, 50 years since 007's first appearance in *Dr No*. To celebrate, a bottle of Macallan 50 year-old is a given a minor starring role in one scene.

Then came that hard-drinking spy, James Bond.
The books by Ian Fleming were laced with whisky,
though it was more often bourbon than Scotch,
possibly because Fleming's doctor allegedly told him
it was healthier than his daily bottle of gin. But when
007 first appeared on screen in *Dr No* in 1962 he
brought with him whisky's nemesis – the base of all
those "shaken not shtirred" Martinis. The triumph
of vodka over whisky is interesting given what was
happening in the spirits market at the time.
Compared to all the ancestral baggage around
Scotch, vodka travelled light as a thoroughly modern
spirit like Bond himself.

Whether the films reflected or led these changes, it
all came down to money, with Smirnoff prepared to
dig deep for its regular guest appearance on screen.
Cynics may wonder if today's script writers simply
type in "Bond orders a drink" every other scene,
with the "drink" auctioned to the highest bidder
from the booze industry. In 2012 Scotch made a
comeback when some Macallan 50-year-old stars in
one brief scene in *Skyfall*. How much its owner, the
Edrington Group, paid is a closely guarded secret.

AWARD-WINNING WHISKY FILM

Far more significant and quite different in tone was
The Angels' Share by Ken Loach, also released in
2012. As in *Whisky Galore!*, Scotland's national drink
takes centre stage in a bittersweet comedy involving
bottles of Irn-Bru and a priceless cask of Maltmill –
the Islay distillery built within the grounds of
Lagavulin.

The distillery operated from 1908 to 1962, though
as far as anyone knows its whisky was never bottled
as a single malt. The film, written by Paul Laverty
and starring first-time actor Paul Brannigan, won
the Jury Prize at Cannes. The whisky writer Charlie
Maclean was hired as consultant and he played
himself in the movie, right down to his monocle and
walrus moustache.

ABOVE Few brands exemplified the postwar
glamour of Scotch whisky better than the 12
year-old deluxe blend of Chivas Regal.

RIGHT Ken Loach's 2012 whisky heist movie was
the first film since *Whisky Galore!* to put Scotch
centre stage. It won that year's jury prize at the
Cannes film festival.

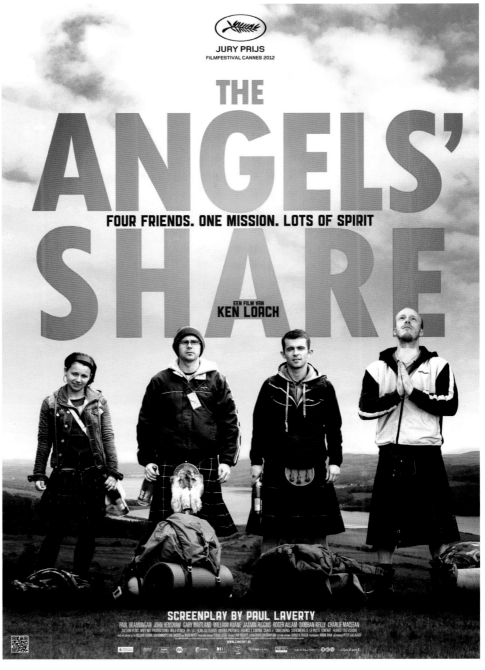

WHISKY IN LITERATURE

"*WHISKEY TO BREAKFAST, WHISKEY TO DINNER, WHISKEY TO SUPPER ...*" BEGINS A BREATHLESS PASSAGE IN *THE UNSPEAKABLE SCOT*, PUBLISHED IN 1902. IT CONTINUES FOR A WHOLE PARAGRAPH: "*... WHISKEY WHEN YOU ARE WELL, WHISKEY IF YOU BE SICK, WHISKEY ALMOST AS SOON AS YOU ARE BORN, WHISKEY THE LAST THING BEFORE YOU DIE – THAT IS SCOTLAND.*" ITS ENGLISH AUTHOR, T.W.H. CROSLAND, WAS LAYING IT ON WITH A TROWEL BECAUSE EVEN IN 1902 THERE WAS MORE TO THE COUNTRY THAN JUST WHISK(E)Y. AS FOR THE EXTRA "E", THAT WAS FAIRLY COMMON AT THE TIME – ITS USE TO DESCRIBE ONLY IRISH AND AMERICAN WHISKEY CAME LATER.

There is a long tradition of visitors to Scotland being struck by the natives' fondness for the water of life and its legendary strength, starting with the intrepid explorer, Martin Martin. On reaching the Isle of Lewis at the end of the seventeenth century, he reported on the life-threatening properties of Usquebaugh Baul which was distilled four times. There is no mention of it in Samuel Johnson's "Journey to the Western Isles of Scotland" of 1775, but he did write that: "A man of the Hebrides ..., as soon as he appears in the morning, swallows a glass of whisky; yet they are not a drunken race, at least I never was present at much intemperance; but no man is so abstemious as to refuse the morning dram, which they call a skalk."

His companion, James Boswell, added that: "Drinking is in reality an occupation which employs a considerable portion of the time of many people, and to conduct it in the most rational and agreeable manner is one of the great arts of living." Johnson confessed to drinking whisky only once, and found it "preferable to any English malt brandy ... [though] what the process was I had no opportunity of enquiring, nor do I wish to improve the art of making poison pleasant".

In *Humphry Clinker*, the picaresque novel of Tobias Smollett published a few years earlier, readers also learned of this mythical spirit "as strong as genever

FAR LEFT Like other observers of Scottish life in the eighteenth century, the author Tobias Smollett was struck by how sober people appeared to be despite the impressive volumes of whisky consumed.

LEFT William McGonagall, the famous teetotal bard of Dundee, never doubted his genius. Despite the laughter his recitals provoked, he earnestly believed he should have been poet laureate.

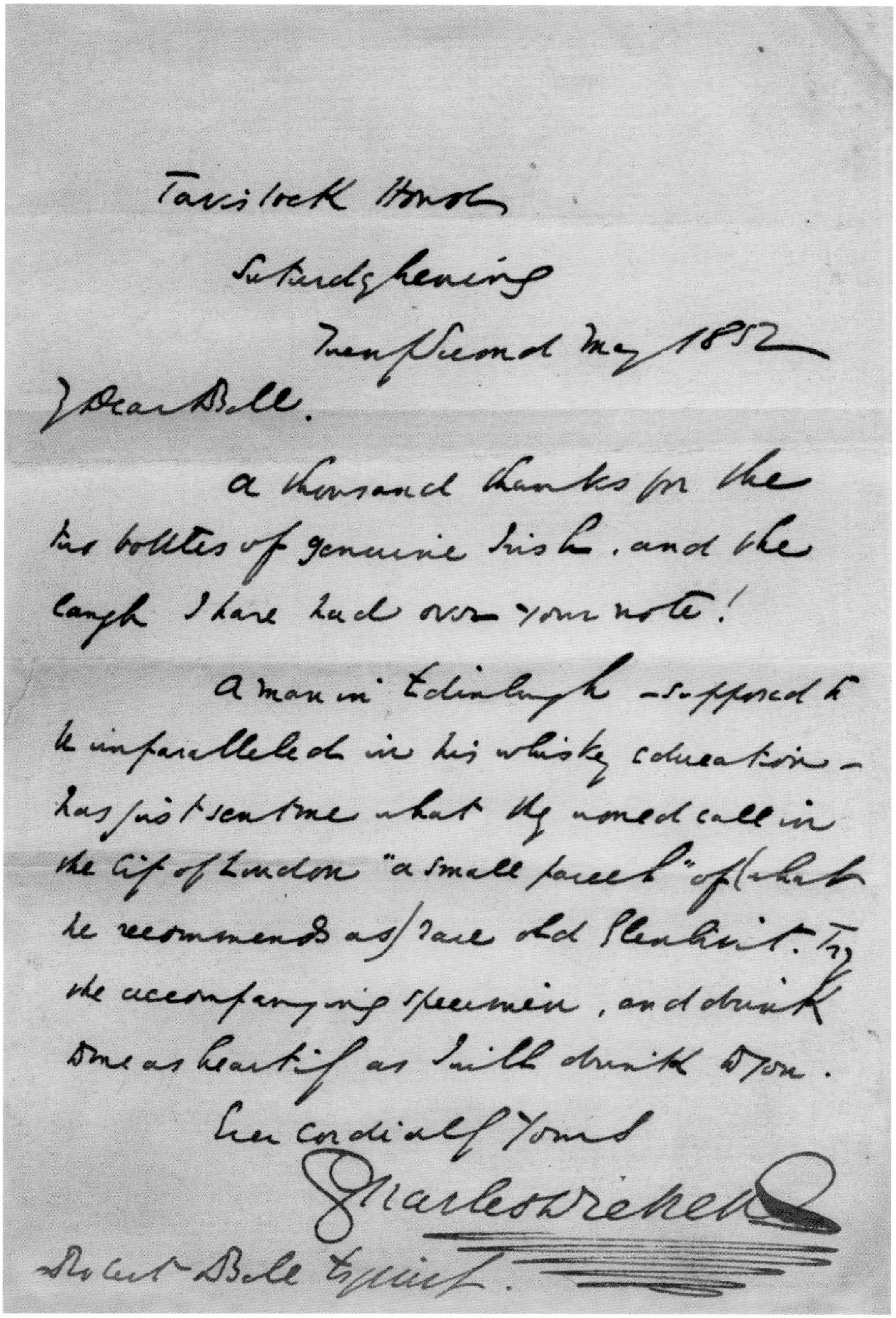

Tavistock House

Saturday Evening

Twenty Second May 1852

My Dear Bell.

a thousand thanks for the two bottles of genuine Irish, and the laugh I have had over your note!

A man in Edinburgh — supposed to be unparalleled in his whiskey education — has just sent me what they would call in the city of London "a small parcel" of what he recommends as rare old Glenlivet. Try the accompanying specimen, and drink some as heartily as I will drink to you.

Ever cordially Yours

Charles Dickens

Robert Bell Esquire.

ABOVE A heartfelt endorsement for "rare old Glenlivet" from Charles Dickens in a letter to a friend in 1852, which ends with the words; "Drink some as heartily as I will drink to you.".

Oh, thou demon Drink, thou fell destroyer;
Thou curse of society, and its greatest annoyer.
What hast thou done to society, let me think?
I answer thou hast caused the most of ills, thou demon
Drink.

[gin] which they [Highlanders] swallow in great quantities without any sign of inebriation. They are used to it from the cradle and find it an excellent preservative against the winter cold, which must be extreme on these mountains." That last point is as true as it ever was.

SUPPORTERS AND OPPONENTS

Rabbie Burns, writing soon afterwards, had no need to inform his readers what whisky was, and his poems delight in the stuff – more for its effect and what it symbolized [*see page* 156]. A century later the tide was turning, and the incomparable William Topaz McGonagall, teetotal poet and tragedian of Dundee, rose to the challenge with "The Demon Drink":

McGonagall was reflecting the popular press, or least the *Daily Mail*. In a ranting, foam-flecked editorial from 1892, it declared of Edinburgh Old Town that: "not in the worst dens of New York can a more brutalised crowd be witnessed. Bareheaded and barefooted women with infants in their arms, uncouth Magdalenes scarred with the leprosy of sin, men on the borderland of delirium tremens ..."

Moving forward a few decades to the other side of the pond, Prohibition helped boost spirits like whisky since given the risks of being caught, you may as well be drinking the hard stuff. It also boosted the criminal underworld who now controlled distribution, and gave birth to a new genre of crime fiction. For America's hard-boiled detective – the antithesis of the English gentleman sleuth – beer was a soft drink for pussies. Real men drank Scotch, either in a tumbler relaxing with a broad, or straight from the bottle in its paper bag.

Love makes the world go round? Not at all. Whisky
makes it go round twice as fast. That's why I'm the most
revolutionary crayture in the whole of Todaidh Mór [this
being Gaelic for the fictional island]

Among countless tales that sprung from and beyond the era of Prohibition was Raymond Chandler's *Farewell My Lovely* from 1940. In one scene his much-parodied hero, Philip Marlowe, is

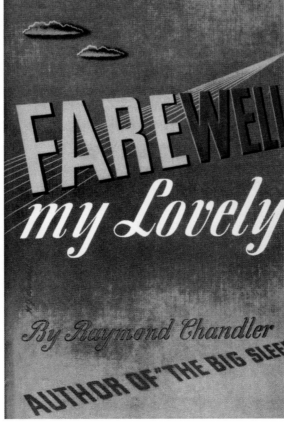

FAR LEFT Graham Greene's novel includes a famous scene where the English hero manages to defeat the sinister Captain Segura in an alcoholic version of draughts where miniature whisky bottles are pitched against other drinks.

LEFT Few writers captured the macho, hard-boiled image of whisky quite like Raymond Chandler.

questioning a suspect: "She poured a fat slug of mellow looking Scotch into my glass, and squirted in some fizz-water. It was the kind of liquor you think you can drink forever, and all you do is get reckless." It was pulp fiction at its finest where whisky was a prop to emphasize the hero's true grit. Caring whether your cocktail was shaken or stirred would have been irredeemably camp. That came later, with a certain spy in the vodka-fuelled adventures of Ian Fleming.

FACT AND FICTION COME TOGETHER

Before then, Scotch enjoyed its moment of fictional glory in Compton Mackenzie's much-loved *Whisky Galore* in 1947. It was inspired by the true tale of the wreck of the SS *Politician* off the Hebridean island of Eriskay. People came from as far as Mull to plunder its cargo of 28,000 cases of Scotch just like the SS *Cabinet Minister* in the book. Having worked for MI6 in Syria, Mackenzie settled on the island of Barra in 1928 and his affection for the islanders and their ingenuity permeates *Whisky Galore*. The spirit fuels the community in the book as the schoolteacher, Norman Macleod, makes distinctly clear when the island is gripped by a terrible whisky drought before the wreck.

Whisky swirls in and out of Graham Greene's novels, notably *The Power and the Glory* (1940) with its flawed "whisky priest" at the centre. There is also a memorable scene featuring miniature bottles of Scotch and a game of draughts in *Our Man in Havana* (1958). While more recently Scottish crime fiction, or Tartan Noir, is steeped in the stuff. Whisky trickles through the pages of Ian Rankin's Inspector Rebus novels, whose hard-drinking hero was particularly fond of Highland Park.

BELOW Raising a dram to the ill-fated SS *Politician* which ran aground here on the Isle of Eriskay on 5 February 1941 and inspired Compton Mackenzie to write the greatest whisky book of all. As well as Scotch, the ship was carrying a vast and unexplained stash of Jamaican bank notes.

WHISKY TOURISM

WHEN QUEEN VICTORIA AND PRINCE ALBERT FIRST STAYED AT BALMORAL IN SEPTEMBER 1848, THEIR NEIGHBOUR, JOHN BEGG, WHO HAD RECENTLY ESTABLISHED THE LOCHNAGAR DISTILLERY NEXT DOOR, INVITED THEM ROUND. THEY DULY APPEARED WITH VARIOUS CHILDREN INCLUDING THE PRINCE OF WALES, THEN AGED SEVEN. BEGG LATER WROTE UP EVERY DETAIL IN HIS DIARY, FROM HOW THEY HAD ALL SIPPED HIS WHISKY TO HOW HE HAD PROVOKED "A VERY HEARTY LAUGH FROM HER MAJESTY". WHAT IS AMAZING, CONSIDERING THE HOOPS OF PROTOCOL YOU WOULD HAVE TO GO THROUGH TODAY, IS THAT BEGG'S INVITATION HAD ONLY BEEN DELIVERED TO BALMORAL THE NIGHT BEFORE.

From this early peak of whisky tourism, distilleries slipped back into the shadows, and 50 years ago the idea of visiting one while on holiday in Scotland would have seemed bizarre. Distilleries did not advertise their presence and their names were little known beyond the workforce, local residents and the whisky blenders. A few had a tiny following among malt whisky connoisseurs, but most were as anonymous as the big grain distilleries still are. The produce of both types of distillery disappeared almost entirely into blended Scotch.

That began to change with the reinvention of single-malt whisky, starting with Glenfiddich in 1963. Six years later the Speyside distillery opened the first ever distillery visitors' centre. Plenty in the industry were sceptical that anyone would want to visit a "factory" while touring the Highlands, but they were wrong. As James Sugden OBE, the former MD of Johnstons of Elgin, the famous textile company, put it: "It's like *Charlie and the Chocolate Factory*. People on holiday want to see other people at work."

BELOW Queen Victoria and Prince Albert picnicking near Balmoral in 1861. Thirteen years earlier they had been among the first whisky tourists in history when they visited the neighbouring distillery of Lochnagar. It was soon calling itself Royal Lochnagar.

LEFT Bruichladdich, on Islay, is one of a number of distilleries which offers tours on almost every day of the year.

BELOW While visiting Scotland why not send a postcard home, like these two early examples, one promoting Usher's famous old vatted Glenlivet, the other neatly linking the perennial Highland Games with one of America's most popular blends.

Highland Games.

As other malt distilleries began laying down stocks to release their own single malts, they realized there was a real interest in provenance among whisky drinkers. It was enough to say "bottled in Scotland" on the label of blended Scotch, but with malts people were curious to learn more. Disused malt barns and floor maltings were converted into visitor centres and shops, as travel companies added distilleries to their list of castles, gardens and battlefields to visit on their bus tours of Scotland. By 2011 some 52 distilleries, almost half the total, were officially open to the public and attracting 1.3 million visitors a year. Meanwhile the rest were drawing a dedicated band of "whisky anoraks" who traipsed around the country bagging far-flung distilleries as others bag Munros (Scottish peaks over 3,000 ft). The more inaccessible and officially closed to visitors they were, the better.

SPREADING THE WORD

As "Scotland in a bottle" Scotch whisky has always helped attract visitors to the country. Single malts have inspired them to delve deeper and discover the source. And, unlike visiting a winery that only springs into life for a few weeks during the harvest, whisky making is a year-round process. It is hard not to be seduced if you experience it in the flesh and see and smell the washbacks fermenting, followed by the sweet scent of spirit radiating from gleaming copper stills. To welcome visitors, show them round and serve them in the distillery shop and café there are now around 650 people employed in whisky tourism in Scotland. In direct terms it may not be a hugely profitable enterprise for the distillers, but if it helps recruit loyal disciples in distant markets who will then spread the word, its benefits are immeasurable.

ABOVE AND LEFT Blends have joined the whisky tourism trail, with Dewar's World of Whisky at Aberfeldy distillery in Perthshire in 2000, soon followed by The Famous Grouse Experience at the tiny Glenturret distillery nearby.

Two well-known blends have followed the same path, starting with Dewar's World of Whisky which sprung up in 2000 beside the brand's spiritual home – the Aberfeldy distillery in Perthshire. With all its archive material and interactive displays, it plays homage to one of the founding fathers of the brand, Tommy Dewar. Two years later and not far away, the tiny Glenturret distillery near Crieff was transformed into The Famous Grouse Experience. It now claims to be one of the top three whisky visitor attractions in the world, but as with Dewar's World of Whisky it can be easy to forget there is actually a malt distillery buried beneath all the heavy branding.

THE SCOTCH WHISKY HERITAGE CENTRE

Before the blends got in on the act, the whisky industry realized it needed some kind of embassy in Edinburgh where people could come and learn about Scotch whisky without having to visit an actual distillery. The nearest, Glenkinchie, is half an hour from the city centre and not so easy to visit without your own car. In 1987, 19 whisky companies invested £2 million each to acquire an abandoned primary school and convert it into the Scotch Whisky Heritage Centre. Right next to Edinburgh Castle, it could hardly have had a better location.

From 70,000 visitors the first year, the Heritage Centre was attracting over a quarter of a million by 2009 when it was given a £3 million face-lift. The highlight of the tour is a Disney-like barrel ride through the whisky-making process. To quote the official description, you will be taken from "gently-swaying fields of barley" past the "steaming and bubbling Pot Still", and finally to the "tick-tock of the passing years of maturation". The tour ends with the world's largest collection of Scotch whisky, some 3,384 bottles amassed by the Brazilian collector Claive Vidiz and bought by Diageo for an undisclosed sum in 2008.

GLASGOW'S OWN

Five years later plans for a similar venture were unveiled for Glasgow, though with a crucial difference. Housed in the old pump house of the Queen's Dock on the Clyde, the Glasgow Distillery Company will produce its own whisky. It will be the first new distillery in the city for over a hundred years, and is the brainchild of Tim Morrison, whose family used to own Morrison Bowmore. Once up and running its still-room will be filled with sweet spirity aromas, making it far more than just another heritage centre.

BELOW LEFT A stone's throw from Edinburgh Castle, the Scotch Whisky Heritage Centre acts as an embassy for the industry, attracting thousands who don't have the time or inclination to visit an actual distillery.

BELOW Tours of the Scotch Whisky Heritage Centre end with the world's biggest whisky collection built up by the Brazilian collector, Claive Vidiz, and sold to Diageo in 2008.

INDEX

174

OPPOSITE Sunrise at Quiraing, on the Isle of Skye.
Both Talisker and Tobhaig come from the Isle
of Skye.

CREDITS

PICTURE CREDITS

The publishers would like to thank the following sources for their kind permission to reproduce the pictures in this book.

AKG Images: /Sotheby's: 74. **Abhainn Dearg:** 76 **The Advertising Archives:** 30TL, 87L, 146, 169BL, 169BR. **Alamy:** /adp-photos: 141T; /William Arthur: 139R; /Bildagentur-online Historical Collection: 25T; /John Bracegirdle: 97B, 121T; /Richard Broadwell: 171L; /Chronicle: 35; /Classic Image: 38L; /Mark Collinson: 122; /Collpicto: 101T; /Marco Cristofori/age fotostock: 89B; /Derek Croucher: 132; /De Agostini/UIG: 101R, 140; /Gary Doak: 156; /Everett Collection: 162L; /Stephen Finn: 93B; /Dario Fusaro/Cephas Picture Library: 30B; /David Gowans: 99B; /Grainger Historical Picture Archive: 166R; /Richard R Handley: 71T; /David Harding: 48-49; /Dennis Hardley: 77T; /Jan Holm: 131B; /Peter Horree: 42T; /Izel Photography – IP3: 98; /Catherine Karnow/Corbis/Flirt: 129B; /Marcus Keller/imageBROKER: 83B; /Elizabeth Leyden: 142; /Lphoto: 170B; /Robin McKelvie: 56; /John McKenna: 107B; /Gordon McManus: 107R; /MediaWorldImages: 47T; /Mirrorpix: 106, 113B, 125T; /Jose Antonio Moreno Castellano/imageBROKER: 80; /David Osborn: 102L, 115L, 115BR; /Colin Palmer Photography: 169T; /John Peter Photography: 127B; /Photos 12: 163B; /Klaus Rainer Krieger/imageBROKER: 58; /Reuters: 127T; /Bertrand Rieger/hemis.fr: 55; /David Robertson: 60; /Kay Roxby: 107T; /Olaf Schubert/imageBROKER: 96; /Scottish Viewpoint: 100, 128, 138; /John Short/Vantage: 44; /South West Images Scotland: 144T; /Phil Steale: 57; /Dave Tacon: 121B; /Tegestology: 176; /travelib: 24R; /United Archives GmbH: 162R; /S Vannini/De Agostini/UIG: 130; /Alan Wilson: 17R. **Auchentoshan:** 150, 151T, 151B. **Bladnoch:** 144B. **Bridgeman Images:** /Historic England: 19; /Universal History Archive/UIG: 18. **Bruichladdich:** 62, 63B, 63R. **Bunnahabhain:** 57T, 69B, 70B. **Burn Stewart:** 71R, 81R. **Campari Group:** 9, 46L, 124, 125BL, 125BR. **Chivas Brothers' Archive:** 23L, 23R, 24L, 30TR, 161T, 165. **Depositphotos:** 99R, 105R, 158-159. **Diageo:** 27T, 27B, 28, 37, 42B, 43B, 78L, 79R, 88L, 88R, 126L, 126R, 145, 148, 149T, 149B. **Edrington Group:** 95R. **Getty Images:** /Mary Ann Anderson/MCT: 91B; /Craig Barritt: 116R; /Bettmann: 7, 26L, 26R, 38R; /Margaret Bourke-White/The Life Picture Collection: 36; /Simon Butterworth: 79B; /Alan Copson: 52; /Alan Cosh: 87R; /Simon Dawson/Bloomberg: 3, 5; /Evening Standard: 157B; /Rocco Fasano: 47B, 114; /Garrett M Graff/MCT: 68, 90; /Tim Graham: 50-51, 72, 81B; /Mark Hamblin: 152-153; /Haywood Magee/Picture Post: 147; /History of Advertising Trust/Heritage Images: 117BR; /Hulton Archive: 34R, 134; /Gary Latham/VisitBritain: 102R, 170T; /John Lawson/Belhaven Moment: 103B; /Matt Mawson/Corbis Documentary: 118; /Jeff J Mitchell: 99T, 105B; /Steven Morris Photography: 66R, 67B; /MyLoupe/UIG: 78R; /NY Daily News: 40; /Walter Nurnberg/Science & Society Picture Library: 86; /Matthew Peyton: 115BL; /Popperfoto: 160; /Peter Ribbeck: 84; /Will Robb: 61B, 70T; /Pete Rowbottom: 110; /Arthur Schatz/The LIFE Images Collection: 31L; /Science & Society Picture Library: 54; /Stock Montage: 157T; /Jeremy Sutton-Hibbert: 94; /TCI/EyeOn/UIG: 12-13, 119B; /Charles Twist: 81T; /UIG: 33, 66L, 108; /Sandro Vannini/Corbis Documentary: 43T, 120; /VisitBritain/Britain on View: 59B. **Glen Scotia:** 135, 137, 141L. **Glenfarclas:** 129R. **Glenfiddich:** 8. **Glenlivet:** 25B, 117R. **Glenrothes:** 123T, 123B. **Harris Distillery:** 77B. **The Irish Historical Picture Company:** 32. **iStockphoto:** 139L, 175. **Laphroaig:** 41R, 64BC, 65B, 65R. **Mary Evans:** 64BR, 155, 164R, 168; /Grosvenor Prints: 17L. **Moray Council Archives and Local Heritage Centre:** 111B. **Morrison Bowmore:** 151R. **Museum of Islay Life:** 71B. **National Library of Scotland:** 20, 45, 75R. **National Records of Scotland:** 15. **Old Pulteney:** 89T, 92L, 92R. **Pernod Ricard:** 116L. **Private Collections:** 34, 59R, 61R, 67R, 69R, 91R, 93R, 97R, 103R, 115R, 119R, 121R, 123R, 125R, 127R, 131R, 149R, 166L. **REX/Shutterstock:** /Associated Newspapers: 29L; /Jim Hutchison/Associated Newspapers: 167; /Studio Canal: 41L, 161B. **Shutterstock:** 46R, 82, 83T, 95T, 97T, 104, 105T, 111T, 113T, 129T, 131T, 136, 154, 163T, 171R. **Springbank:** 141R. **Superstock:** /imageBROKER: 101B. **Topfoto:** 29R, 39, 112, 117BL, 164L; /Barnes: 14; /City of London/HIP: 22T; /Houghton: 95B; /Land Lost Content/HIP: 31R **Unsplash:** /Sandra Ollier: 10-11. **Whyte & Mackay:** 83R. **Wikimedia Commons:** 16T, 16B, 21L, 21R, 22B, 75L.

Every effort has been made to acknowledge correctly and contact the source and/or copyright holder of each picture and Carlton Books Limited apologises for any unintentional errors or omissions that will be corrected in future editions of this book.

176

PUBLISHERS' ACKNOWLEDGMENTS

The Publishers would like to thank the following people and organisations for their help in providing information, images and other material for this book: Christine McCafferty at Diageo plc; Alison Morris and Eleanor Kidd at Elgin Library and Moray Council Archives; Jim Long and Chris Brousseau at the Chivas Brothers' Archive and Pernod-Ricard; Alice at Mail Marketing (Scotland) Ltd on behalf of Laphroaig; The National Library of Scotland; and Dr Stephanie Metze and Tessa Spencer at the National Records of Scotland.